caressa

caressa
From Call Girl to God's Child

The True Story of a Psychic Prostitute

Ken Llewelyn

First published in Australia by
Sandstone Publishing
Unit 1, 360 Norton Street
Leichhardt NSW 2040

© Ken Llewelyn 2002

All rights reserved. No part of this publication may be reproduced, stored in a retrieval system, or transmitted in any form or by any means, electronic, mechanical, photocopying, recording or otherwise, without the prior written permission of the publisher and the copyright holder.

National Library of Australia Cataloguing-in-Publication entry:
Llewelyn, Ken.
Caressa: from call girl to God's child.
Bibliography.
ISBN 1 86505 431 3.
1.Fleming, Liz. 2. Prostitutes – Australia – Biography.
I.Title

306.742092

Cover & text design: ljdesign.
Cover photgraph: © Image100 Ltd
Internal photographs: Tony Healy, Ken Llewelyn
Printed in Australia by McPhersons Printing Group, Victoria.
54321   04 03 02

preface

When medium Monica Hamers told me I should meet a Canberra-based prostitute to investigate 'spirit messages' left on her 'love tapes' I could not have been more sceptical. It took me more than three months before I could be persuaded to visit Liz Fleming. Even on our first meeting I was not impressed; I agreed to a second meeting only because of my close friendship with Monica.

From that second meeting I quickly became enmeshed in Liz's extraordinary life. She was a woman who liked to live life on the edge, whether it was the extremes of prostitution or challenging spirit forces to do her bidding. Let me be candid: this book is often brutal in exposing the extremes of Liz's trade. Yet I believe she has provided an outlet for men whose perversions would appal many. Further, how many women has she saved from rape or other physical attack? How many innocents has she prevented from being scarred for life? Even for Liz, a mother of two, play acting for a man who wanted her to say, 'Daddy, Daddy don't hurt me!' was not easy.

Liz was fascinated by the 'spirit world'. To her, the spirits were real, and, at times, she appeared to be able to direct and control spirit forces as though they were visible on the earth plane. Many of the stories told in this book might seem preposterous, but before you judge listen to the witnesses—not only to Liz's story but also to the remarkable poltergeist case of Humpty Doo, near Darwin.

So, why did I write this book? Yes, it is sensational and many readers will be shocked by the content. But I urge you to read on to the end: there is hope and spiritual fulfilment to come. Liz provided me with a vehicle to emphasise the importance of personal responsibility, the universal law of cause and effect, and finally spiritual evolution.

I believe that one day it will be proved that we live many lives. That each life takes us a little further along the spiritual track, however many times we deviate or demur. Only when we have this understanding will we genuinely respect and nurture our own lives as well as the lives of all others on our long-suffering planet.

Ken Llewelyn
July 2002

special notes

The author stresses that this book does not in any way present, nor does it intend to present, the official view of the paranormal held by the Royal Australian Air Force or the Department of Defence.

Further, because of the nature of the material in this book, most of Liz Fleming's friends and witnesses requested that they be given pseudonyms.

contents

Preface v
1 Beyond belief 1
2 Early experiences of sex and spirits 13
3 Ghostly antics in brothels 23
4 Masturbation to prostitution 33
5 Caressa and her clients 49
6 Prostitution through the centuries 75
7 An evening with the gods 89
8 Extraordinary witness reports 101
9 Amazing happenings at Humpty Doo 121
10 Seeking solutions: riding on the edge 151
11 Supporting evidence 167
12 Caressa has the final word 187
13 For Liz suicide brings enlightenment 191
Bibliography 203

1
beyond belief

I didn't believe the outrageous claims made by Canberra prostitute Liz Fleming until I saw a cigarette lighter fly gently through the air in front of me, apparently without any natural physical force applied, and—incredibly—light in mid-air!

When I first visited Liz, in October 1994, she excitedly told me about the strange goings-on in her life, among them spirit messages transposed over her 'love tapes'. The tapes had been specially recorded to relax Liz's clients and put them in the right mood. Liz insisted that I listen to the ghostly recorded messages, at the same time bombarding me with other amazing stories. To be honest, I thought she was on drugs: she spoke so quickly and with such fervour. Besides, I had been researching psychic phenomena for more than 15 years and her story was way over the top. And, after listening to the tapes with considerable scepticism, I decided it wouldn't have been too difficult for someone with only limited acting aptitude to record the messages.

I spent five years researching the 'Liz Fleming case' and visited the bubbly prostitute many times. I also interviewed nine outsiders—

from her hairdresser to a social worker, who visited her professionally—and all told stories that defied logic and did much to confirm my own observations. One of these outsiders was a 55-year-old construction worker who is still wondering how his keys, locked accidentally inside his truck, were 'thrown by an invisible force' into Liz's bedroom after they had had sex.

* * *

I was introduced to Liz through a close friend, medium Monica Hamers, who thought I would be interested in the spirit messages. Before meeting Liz, I checked the classifieds in the *Canberra Times*: in between 'Angie, passionate, pampering and provocative' and 'Desirable buxom young blonde, loves to party' was 'Beautiful Caressa, available my home by appointment'. Beautiful Caressa ... I wondered if the words were true? We arranged to meet late one Sunday night in October.

I had trouble finding Liz's small suburban house, which was surrounded by jasmine and native shrubs, and it was around 10.30 when I finally parked my old Subaru. Monica and Liz were already talking animatedly about the spirit messages. Liz—or, to use her professional name, Caressa—was quite short, with dyed curly blonde hair and a pretty face, but I could not fail to notice her most alluring qualities, even though I was recovering from a viral infection and felt rotten. I was actually having trouble working up some enthusiasm for this meeting, and the thought of trudging off to work the next day was an added deterrent. But Liz, with her infectious personality, kept me engaged despite my unwillingness to listen to things that at the time I considered a sham.

So I dutifully listened to the spirit messages on the tapes. Unfortunately for Liz, the more I heard the more sceptical I became: in between pop stars, such as Whitney Houston belting out a hit from her *Bodyguard* album, were dead spots filled with strange whisperings and muffled voices. My frustration grew, but I listened to the tapes another three times and then gladly took my leave around midnight. Perhaps the lateness of the hour and the thought of an early start on Monday were uppermost in my mind. I thought the evidence was very shaky. Because of my friendship with Monica, though, I told Liz I would return to pursue the matter. I wasn't hopeful of anything unusual.

On my subsequent visits to Liz's house in late 1994 the array of phenomena displayed in my presence was startling. Certainly, rock throwing, the smashing of glass by unseen forces, and the manifesting of objects is relatively common in the literature on the paranormal but I failed to find a case similar to this during my many hours of research in libraries in Australia and overseas. Even parapsychologists Professor David Fontana, from Cardiff University, and Professor Bob Morris, head of the Department of Parapsychology at Edinburgh University, could not readily recall research into psychic phenomena involving a prostitute. Professor Fontana, who is also president of the prestigious Society of Psychical Research, had, however, written a paper discussing the interesting case of an 'intelligent' poltergeist in Cardiff, which I discuss in Chapter 11.

In spite of the fact that I had written *Flight into the Ages*, a controversial book containing some amazing material about paranormal activities in the Air Force, nothing compared with the direct evidence of 'invisible forces' surrounding Liz Fleming. Even the seven days I spent in the Philippines watching and experiencing stunning feats of psychic surgery paled into insignificance in the face of the evidence I gathered during my research into Liz's 'spirit friends'. In the Philippines the psychic forces were activated through the 'surgeon's hands'; the forces surrounding Liz were bizarre and unpredictable. Ironically, she believed these forces were not only real but that they provided her with genuine comfort in a profession known to cause the strongest of women to wither.

After lengthy discussions with Liz, and before I began my research in earnest, we agreed to three rules.

First, we agreed that this book would represent her life as a prostitute. As time went by and I became more familiar with Liz and her profession, I realised that not only did she attract spirit forces; her clients had 'fetishes' that were equally weird. Perhaps there was a connection. It soon became clear that the psychic phenomena that had become such an integral part of Liz's existence could not be ignored.

The second rule was that there was to be no sex between us. Liz admits to paying, with her body, construction workers, carpet layers, even a legal adviser. Some of her regular clients said she was the best and she wanted me to be convinced too, but it is important to stress that at no time have I been Liz's client or received sexual favours from her.

We all know prostitution is a hard game. You have to make your money while your body remains desirable. There is neither pension scheme nor sickness benefit. Daily you are subjected to what most of us would regard as degrading experiences. Always there is the danger of being bashed. Liz has had her share of physical abuse yet, remarkably, she remained in most respects mentally unscathed and indeed insists that prostitution gave her self-respect and probably saved her from committing suicide.

The third, and most important, rule concerned the truth. I told Liz that if I found she was trying to dupe me in any way I would drop the story. I learnt to respect Liz's integrity: she was also adamant that the story should be truthful.

So this book is about Liz and two subjects that, although not taboo, are not generally aired for public consumption—prostitution and psychic phenomena. We have Liz the prostitute who, as her fellow hookers say, goes further than any other prostitute they know. As she said to me in her characteristically direct way, 'I love what I do and I know I'm fucking good at it.' And we have Liz the psychic who tempts fate—and goodness knows what else—by playing dangerous games with spirit forces.

Finally, I believe it is important that readers 'know' Liz the person. As a result, in a number of the chapters that follow Liz is quoted at length.

I agreed to meet Liz again on the evening of 17 November 1994. Her friend Donna, who occasionally acts as her receptionist, was also going to be there. As I rode my Triumph motorbike the 20 or so kilometres to her home I had to acknowledge my scepticism. But, then again, the weather was pleasant and I always enjoy a ride, so there was nothing to lose. I felt very relaxed by the time I entered the house.

The sight of Donna chain-smoking was disconcerting, though, and she quickly volunteered that she was terrified of communing with Liz's spirits, yet for some reason always wanted to try again. She spoke hurriedly in a nervous, staccato manner of experiences she'd had as a brothel receptionist—phones ringing with 'ghostly voices' on the end of the line; a baseball bat that appeared from 'nowhere' and smashed into a wall; even a palm tree reefed out of its holder and thrown at her feet. She also claimed that in a previous session with Liz she had been belted across the face by an unseen 'hand', which left a large red welt. Liz explained that Donna's presence was important because it provided extra 'power' for the spirits.

I still felt uncomfortable and wondered whether the two of them had been taking drugs. But Donna's nervousness did seem genuine, contrasting oddly with Liz's obvious excitement at what might eventuate. As I watched Liz I could understand why she was so popular with clients. Just over 150 centimetres tall, she exuded a concentrated nervous energy; her hazel eyes shone with anticipation and her strong, effervescent personality dominated the conversation. Liz always made a strong visual impact on men. Her long blond hair loosely covering the straining lacy bra only added a sense of beguiling mystery.

The evening's entertainment soon began. As Liz and Donna regaled me with more and more 'crazy' stories I began to hear loud banging on the walls. I listened carefully but could not determine the source. I thought Liz and Donna might be tricking me, having organised a friend to thump on the walls. Yet the thumping wasn't restricted to one room, and it was impossible to tell where the next thump would come from. I still wasn't convinced, though, so I looked around the rooms and even outside the house. I found neither physical presences nor a simple explanation. Later, a construction worker told me he had heard similar thumps before having sex with Liz. It was as though whoever or whatever it was wanted to provide an appropriate introduction to the coming events.

As Liz, Donna and I sat around the kitchen bench chatting I saw the first peculiar thing. Nothing major—just half a lipstick holder thrown off the kitchen table onto the floor. Other items quickly followed—a safety pin, a hair clip, three throat lozenges from the adjacent bench, a pen, and finally the lipstick holder ... again. There appeared to be no external force. No strings, no strong wind, just the objects thrown off the kitchen benches. I was curious, but still not convinced. I wondered whether it was sleight of hand or some other sort of conjuring trick.

Liz, meanwhile, seemed unimpressed with such 'small time' activity and insisted we move to the bedroom, where she believed something more interesting would happen. Being asked into a prostitute's bedroom with another woman would invariably raise salacious comment.

My thoughts about this were temporally diverted as Liz once again played the taped spirit messages. After another 10 minutes or thereabouts it was obvious to her that I was still sceptical, so she stopped the recorder and rewound the cassette back to zero. Then the three of us went to her bedroom.

Liz's bedroom is designed to give clients the right ambience. Mood lighting is provided by a low-wattage red light in the ceiling and three floor lamps—two touch lamps and another one with subdued red lighting. (On the two nights when poltergeist activity took place in the bedroom there was a high-wattage white bulb in the ceiling light, enabling me to observe the activity clearly.) The visuals in the bedroom were enhanced by pictures: a bikie shot of a nude girl across a red Harley Davidson; a very sexy shot of a girl 'dressed' in a white teddy, with white stockings, garters and suspenders; and one of a young couple, fully dressed, embracing on a lounge with six puppies staring at them.

Liz's 'work area' is a normal double bed; a red sheet (satin for special occasions) covers the 'extra-strength' mattress and two large sheepskin-covered 'boomerang supports' lie beside the normal red pillows. The room is insulated with a very heavy padded curtain—not only to keep prying eyes out but also to allow clients the freedom to vocally enjoy the pleasure of the moment without complaints from the neighbours. On the thick shag-pile carpet is an audio recorder with tapes of Liz's special love music. Adjacent is a box containing enough condoms for a regiment and a black vibrator big enough to accommodate the most outrageous appetite. And if Liz needs support for her seduction technique she can always resort to the porn loaded in the video recorder, conveniently placed in the corner of the bedroom. Climate control is provided with a powerful heater on one side of the bed and a cooler on the other. Unless the bedroom door is open there is not a skerrick of fresh air. Two artificial plants—the real ones died from lack of fresh air—complete the decor. Perhaps asphyxiation is an aphrodisiac.

I was relieved that no attempt was made to seduce me. Liz and Donna simply made themselves comfortable on the bright red coverlet directly opposite me. Regardless, I took the opportunity to thoroughly check the bedroom, to see if there were any signs of wires or strings or even someone hidden under the bed or in the cupboard. I found nothing to make me suspicious. Although I knew the front door was closed I admit someone could have quietly entered the house without me knowing. Finally, I sat down on a small cane chair opposite the bed and Liz switched off the lights. This put me on guard immediately, but we just sat quietly and waited.

Within minutes there was a crash and something landed at my feet. Liz yelled and turned on the lights. There on the floor in front of me was a coathanger, which Liz swore had been in the closed cupboard moments before. Could the pair have 'created' the right moment? I wasn't sure, but I am sure of what happened next. As we spoke I watched a cigarette lighter flying gently through the air and—wait for it—light in mid-air! The extraordinary thing about this was that the lighter remained vertical, as though carried very slowly by an invisible hand. And not only was the lighter vertical, so was the flame, which moved as though 'protected' by an air pocket.

This was the first phenomenon that really caught my attention. Liz and Donna did not see the flight of the lighter because it appeared behind their backs, in front of the blacked-out window. All I can say is that the lighter came from the direction of the built-in closed cupboard, starting at a height of about a metre and a half, flying a couple of metres, and then losing power and landing on the bedroom floor. I was, to say the least, surprised.

When I told them what I'd witnessed Liz became very excited, and even more so when Donna picked up the lighter and said it was hers. She said she had left it on the kitchen table, which really confused matters. If the lighter had 'flown in' from the kitchen it must have passed through a wall and a closed door. Not possible. I thought at the time a mechanism could have been set up to throw the lighter but I could see no evidence of this. And if that had been the case, how had the flame been activated? Later, at home, I flicked on a lighter and moved it through the air. Unless this is done very slowly, the flame goes out; besides, the flame I had seen at Liz's remained vertical in spite of the horizontal movement.

We continued sitting in the bedroom, waiting quietly for another 45 minutes or so, but in spite of Liz's frequent exhortations to her spirit friends nothing else happened. Dejected, Liz led the way into the kitchen. Suddenly she turned around to me, shouting with excitement and pointing to the tape recorder, which had the 'play' and 'record' buttons activated. I was absolutely certain the machine had been turned off when we left the kitchen for the bedroom. Convinced a message had been recorded, Liz quickly pushed the 'stop' button, rewound the tape and pressed 'play'. As the tape moved slowly through the cassette the same weird voices I had heard previously came through, but as we listened more carefully something else became quite audible: 'Where are you, Ken?'

Liz could scarcely contain herself—to her, this was solid proof again. And I was completely perplexed. I was certain there was no one else in the house and I was certain the tape recorder had been wound back to zero and stopped before we entered the bedroom. Or was I wrong? Did Liz have an accomplice who planted the tape while we were in the bedroom? Yes, it was not impossible, but, because of evidence I gathered at later sessions, third-party involvement seemed highly improbable. It was all very confusing: the evidence I had just been confronted with suggested that Liz's chortlings about spirit messages may very well be right and that the 'voice' was put there by an unknown psychic presence that also had sufficient power to activate the 'play' and 'record' buttons.

But what really fascinated me was the appearance of the cigarette lighter. Mine was not the only case involving the inexplicable movement of a lighter. In *Modern Psychic Experiences* Joe Cooper describes the story of a woman named Susan, whose lighter frequently disappeared and was always found at the bottom of a zipped-up handbag. Similarly, she found at the bottom of her handbag a set of keys that had been hanging on the wall. Science tells us it is impossible for solid objects to pass through solid walls.

Yet in psychic literature the phenomenon of objects being transported from distant locations, through solid objects, has been reported. These objects—usually referred to as 'apports' (from the French *apporter*, which means 'to bring')—must be de-materialised and re-materialised for the transfer to take place. Is it possible to transform matter to energy and vice versa? By the time I finished my research I was becoming convinced.

* * *

As an aside, I recall discussing with Air Commodore Tom Trinder (retired) a ball of electrical plasma that passed through the windscreen of his aircraft. The incident occurred on 13 September 1963 over Gold River, north of Vancouver, while Tom was flying a

Lockheed Neptune during an exchange posting with the Canadians. Storms in the area were severe and a lightning strike blew up an oil storage tank at Gold River. Inside the Neptune, the crew was suffering from severe turbulence, which was exacerbated by St Elmo's fire—a phenomenon caused by the build-up of static electricity and producing the visual effect of thousands of charged particles, like a fluorescent wool rug. Tom told me,

> 'A strong lightning strike caused an enormous bang on the front antenna. I saw a big ball of electrical plasma pass through the windscreen and land on my lap. It just sat there glowing, spreading over an area more than 15 centimetres each side of my legs. Then it slid off my lap and rolled down the middle of the aircraft. Some of it went out through the drift meter and welded part of the meter to the airframe. The remainder continued rolling down the fuselage, setting fire to the ditching straps, and finally out through the tail, where it burnt the last 3 metres of the anti-collision light cabling and blew the anti-collision light and fibreglass support off the tail. I had been concentrating so hard on the instruments that I only saw the ball of green electrical discharge through my peripheral vision. The other pilot and engineer were blinded for more than a minute.'

Dr Andrew Davies, a scientist with the Department of Defence, has a particular interest in electrical phenomena. During a break in a seminar we attended in August 1995, he told me of a case where a ball of electrical plasma 'walked' along a shelf, 'pushing' over china display plates. Interestingly, he did not dismiss the possibility of the cigarette lighter passing through a solid wall if a 'fourth dimension exists'.

The evening at Liz's had been of great interest, but I was still very concerned that I had been duped. If what I had witnessed was genuine, then it appeared the psychic force had an 'intelligence' and, indeed, enjoyed playing games. This was different from anything I had previously encountered, which made it even more difficult to think about it rationally—was I in fact the subject of a clever conjuring trick? I'm sure the internationally renown sceptic James Randi would support this view.

Liz was concerned that I did not share her enthusiasm about the night's events. But my lukewarm response was prompted by caution and the need to reflect on what had happened. I had read about or been told of similarly strange events, although I concluded that some of the more outrageous cases I had studied were 'engineered bullshit' designed to sell books or magazines. I needed more evidence, so we arranged another meeting in December.

It was time to leave. As I walked down her driveway Liz bombarded me with more 'evidence' while Donna cautioned me about the dangers of the powers that she had seen unleashed in her presence. I pulled on my helmet and jabbed the starter of my 900cc Triumph, the throb of the powerful triple giving me a sense of comfort and familiarity. I left the visor up to allow the air to clear my brain as I mulled over the past three hours. With 100 bhp on tap, the Trident is difficult to keep under the speed limit, but that night 100 kph was fast enough.

My leisurely progress along the Monaro Highway allowed time for enjoying the cool evening air and the unique smells of the Australian bush. Normally I keep a very close eye on my mirrors, to check for police: this time I was vaguely aware of a set of lights staying about 200 metres behind me, but my mind was elsewhere. Sure enough, as I turned off the dual carriageway a police car shot past. They must have been following me for the last 5 kilometres, waiting for me to rip open the throttle and let those thirsty Mikuni carburettors unleash the bike into the licence-losing zone. I gave it little thought at the time, except to wonder why they would waste their time following a bike on a deserted dual carriageway: was it revenue-raising or a couple of young cops interested in the possible thrill of chasing a high-performance bike. Whatever. Little did I know that next time Liz's spirit friends would take more than a passing interest in the Triumph; it was then that I started to understand why Donna showed such fear of these unseen forces.

At home, I slumped into my reclining chair, lit a cigarette and opened a Cascade—the Tasmanian beer I had developed a taste for during my six-month secondment in that State with the Australian Broadcasting Corporation. I leant back, blew smoke rings towards the ceiling, and dwelt on what might happen next time.

In retrospect, the evening had had a big impact on me. I guess it was similar to when, as a student pilot with the Royal Air Force, I flew a jet for the first time, low over the Yorkshire Moors. That first low-level flight in a Jet Provost was in essence an ethereal experience, clearly imprinted on my mind. My relationship with Liz was also important, yet I knew it was only a small part of my continued delving into the unknown. But the house was strange, Liz was strange, and Donna was terrified. Where did I fit in? Was I destined to cross the path of this intelligent, sensual woman with a penchant for penetrating sexual and psychic boundaries? I didn't know.

Early experiences of sex and spirits

Born in Melbourne in 1955, Liz had a difficult upbringing. She hated kindergarten and school and had an 'abrasive' relationship with her parents, especially her father. She felt unloved, unwanted and isolated, often being left unattended by her parents, who were shift workers. As she grew older, self-gratification through sexual pleasure filled a void and became the opiate she needed to blot out the dreadful experiences she had with her father when she was child.

'In a very sick way, I returned this cruelty to my father when he was very ill in 1978,' she recalled without emotion.

> 'While he lay helpless in the lounge room, just to spite him I read to him my own 'death notice'. I hated him so much I had made up my own obituary, knowing that it would hurt him, like he hurt me. I'm not proud of what I did, but why should I be sorry when he started to cry? He used to belt me like you wouldn't believe, over little things, like my legs raised over the heater to keep warm. Even at a tender age I tried to persuade my mother to leave him. I was a very sad and confused adolescent.

Here is one example of how cruel my father could be. My mum, my adopted brother—who suffered from epilepsy and severe emotional disturbances—and I huddled in the corner of a bedroom while my father lit matches and threw them at us. We were petrified, burying our heads in each other's bodies, cowering in fear. To this day, my mother's screams haunt me, yet she still denies my father might have been unstable. To show his mental confusion here is another example. He tried to open a locked bedroom door by pouring boiling water into the keyhole. We were hiding in the bedroom to escape his wrath yet again.

I often reflect on his behaviour and still cannot understand his twisted mind. If my mother made him a beautiful meal, it was frequently thrown from one end of the room to another. Yet she would immediately cook him another, only for my father to do it all over again. Even holidays were unhappy. I still recall the arguments: Mum and Dad were always at loggerheads. Going for a drive in the car was never pleasant as Dad would stop at every pub to have a 'raspberry', as I was told.

In fact, I don't really remember any reasonable conversations my parents had. Most of the time dad didn't communicate; he just stared into space, smoking cigarettes and drinking beer. There was never any affection between them, not even so much as calling each other pet names. Dad's way of getting Mum's attention was by banging on the walls and she would immediately respond to his demands. In my own mind I was a prisoner and had lost all control over my life, as well as over my emotions.

Naturally, as a young girl I wanted to know where babies came from. All Mum said was, 'When you grow up I'll tell you all about it.' Later she gave me a book called *You're a Woman Now*—I was horrified and embarrassed by the contents. She told me about a thing you get called 'your periods', but I was warned never to repeat our conversation to anybody because it was a very big secret and nobody ever talked about it. My ignorance caused me no end of problems ... I was educated by picking up gossip around the school. One young girl, who worked at a horse-racing stables, had the reputation of being a 'turkey-gobbler'. I knew it must have been something sexual because everybody was whispering about it, but I had no idea what it meant. More gossip surrounded a classmate who had been 'fingered'. I wondered what that meant. I read in magazines about this thing you insert inside your vagina, where it says no more pads, no wetness, invisible, all that sort of thing. I thought to myself, 'Where does it go?' I didn't know you had a hole up there to put it in.

When I started to menstruate I was too scared to tell my mother, so I used to put tissues there. When I finally got the courage to tell her I thought I had my periods all she said was, 'You're a woman now.' I nearly died with embarrassment because my problems stemmed from not wanting to grow up ... I didn't want to grow old. When she called me a 'woman' that was the worst name I could have ever been called. I wasn't ashamed of being a female, just very embarrassed that I was developing into a woman. She wanted me to wear a bra, suspenders and high heels, just like she did, and I cringed with revulsion knowing that I was now a woman. Mum never discussed the subject of sex again. In reality, I was really uneducated about the subject until I became a prostitute.

I lost my virginity at the Cheltenham Park cemetery one Friday night with a 12-year-old kid named Pat. I knew he was going to fuck me but I didn't know where they put it or what they did with it. I just lay there beside the headstones, without knickers, with my legs spread. I could see his very small erection, but it was all over in seconds. I was told at school that sex was supposed to be beautiful: I didn't know what all the fuss was about. I didn't feel a thing. Besides Pat was no fool. He knew he was onto a good thing and he wanted to be popular. The following Friday night he brought about 12 of his mates along and I had my first 'gang-bang' a week after losing my virginity. I was only 14 and didn't have a clue about the risks or consequences of sexual intercourse. I thought babies came out of your belly button. Again, the experience meant little. I can't even remember whether they had erections or not; all I can remember was that I bled and my body was covered with mosquito bites as a result of cavorting around the cemetery with 'only my socks on', as the rumours later suggested! At the time I reasoned it was going to be worth it because at last I too was going to be popular—just like my more attractive girlfriends.

Soon word got around the suburb that I was 'easy' and boys would stand outside the front of my home and wait for me. They even phoned my father, and when he said 'Don't ever call here again' I heard them yelling over the telephone 'She fucks like a rattle snake.' It wasn't surprising that I quickly became known as a 'tart' and, to show you how foolish I was, I thought being named a tart was great. I did in fact become very, very popular.

It was so wonderful to be liked, but it was short lived. Later they turned around and hated me, and called me a slut. I can't tell you how much that hurt. Anyway as a consequence I developed an obsessive guilty conscience, which quickly turned to self-hate. From being someone, suddenly I was a nothing, a nobody. I wanted to be beautiful like my girlfriends, some of whom became models. When I look back I'm still envious. I had nothing, except increasingly unhealthy obsessions, and a love for the horses I used to ride. Horses responded to me; they didn't worry how I looked. I was numbed from the unexpected hostility and venom that arose from those two sexual experiences. In fact, it could have resulted in my not feeling anything from relationships until I was well into my thirties.

Following those experiences at school, it was quite some

time before I had any sexual contact with boys. Not surprisingly, I became a prude and sex became a solitary business. I loved to tease but refused to let them fuck me. Even during my teens and twenties I had few relationships, partly because I developed an eating disorder.

Worse was to come. I was prescribed Valium when I was 16, but drugs did not help my emotional problems. I also developed bulimia and at 18 I saw my first psychiatrist. He gave me a book to read, *Relief without Drugs*, which of course was of little help. Between the ages of 18 and 21, I received at least 40 electroconvulsive therapy treatments, but nothing worked because of my deep-rooted resentment. I believed I was repulsive, grotesque and worthless. Finally, I was admitted to hospital, where I became totally obsessed with my lack of perfection, in both body and mind. I didn't want to live because there was nothing to live for. I remember doctors telling my mother, when I was 21, that I would be institutionalised for life if I didn't come to terms with my appearance and drop my obsession with my weight. They all thought I was psychotic and prescribed many medications and intensive psychotherapy. All I wanted was to be kept in a lock-up so that I didn't have to face the world, myself or my body. It was years before I had the courage to look at my naked body. I used to close my eyes as I took my clothes off— even now I still can't look at myself in mirrors. This enormous self-hate has caused me to attempt suicide many times in my life.

Much of this hate could have stemmed from my relationship with my parents and ill-health as a child. I was continually in and out of the Children's Hospital in Melbourne, with rheumatic fever, which damaged my heart. My schoolwork was affected; worse than that, I felt lonely and unloved because I was forced to stay in bed for hours without company or even a television. I spent my twenty-first birthday in a psychiatric ward.

My life revolved around food, and nobody was surprised as I swung between anorexia and bulimia. Nevertheless, while in care, and in spite of my physical state, I seemed to gain great comfort from sex. It was something I could turn to when the rest of my life was so fucked up, so it too became an obsession. At the age of 21 I came under the care of a gorgeous psychiatrist who was a medical superintendent at a well-known psychiatric hospital. He questioned my sexual behaviour and asked me if I masturbated. 'Yes' I told him reluctantly. I can remember him saying to me at the time, 'Do you fantasise?' I replied 'No' because I didn't know what fantasising meant. He explained, 'Do you ever think of erotica or something that turns you on?' I thought about it after I left his rooms and went home to masturbate and fantasise to see what it felt like. I remember my very first fantasy: it was with Rod Stewart and we were 'sixty-nining' each other as I blasted his music on my stereo!

It was only about three years ago that Mum sent me a press clipping from Melbourne outlining charges made against that psychiatrist for sexual harassment involving a patient. I was sorry to read that he had been struck off the medical register, both in Australia and overseas. He was a leader in his field and was recognised as being a 'psychiatrist's psychiatrist'. I remember him giving me a cuddle and I wished he had gone further. I wouldn't have complained. Considering my chosen profession, it still amazes me, and others, that I didn't have intercourse with men from the age of 16 until I was about 24. I fooled around but no penetration. I always had large, beautiful breasts and was called 'Luscious Liz' by a group of guys that I lived with.

Then marriage. I met my first husband when I was 23. He was 28. I told him I was a virgin and he believed me because I wouldn't let him fuck me for six months. After a proper courtship, I finally consented to spend a weekend away with him in the small town of Harden in New South Wales. That was the first time he screwed me. Not surprisingly, after we had romped around the bedroom drinking champagne, I became pregnant. Luckily, I didn't get pregnant when I was fucking around as a kid.

My first unusual experience occurred when my marriage was breaking down. By this time I had two boys and the 3-year-old was giving me trouble. The day-nursery told me he should be removed. He was such a disruption to the other kids—even when he was six months old the carer had refused to look after him because of his behaviour. These difficulties were made even worse by the fact that there was no love between my husband and me, just an attachment. Our relationship had progressively deteriorated, and the problems were compounded by my bulimia. I wanted to escape and leave my family: I knew if I stayed it would only deepen my children's unhappiness.

Very early one morning I was lying on my side. I could see the daylight filtering through the curtains and, in spite of my disturbed mental state, I was unusually relaxed. Suddenly I became aware of an intense vibration shaking my body: I felt as though I was speeding through a tunnel at a million miles an hour towards a distant bright light. The experience frightened me and instantly I returned to my body. I was thankful to return to my normal state. Within seconds, though, I found myself speeding through the tunnel once again, so I decided to let go and travel a little further. Still I was apprehensive, and soon managed to pull myself away again.

But I am always interested in new sensations, so when it happened a third time, which seemed like only seconds later, I was ready to go even further through this tunnel towards the light. I let myself surrender and found it to be the most beautiful, peaceful experience of my life. This time I felt no fear. I was disappointed when I could go no further towards the bright light: I wanted to see what was beyond it. Maybe I was only allowed to experience this much.

Unfortunately, I was never able to repeat that wonderful experience. I did, however, manage to delve in another direction and sometimes my body would 'lift and float' around my bedroom while physically I lay on my back. I appeared to be on another level of consciousness. And I often felt my 'body' levitate when I was lying on my stomach, and it concerned me that I was unable to control these sensations. None of these experiences was induced through drugs.

Eventually I contacted a lady from Eckankar [a US-based organisation whose members believe in the possibility of spiritual experiences] and she said, 'Oh Liz, you've come of age. You're having your first experiences.' I didn't know what the hell she was talking about but I wanted to learn more. Being unhappily married and unable to leave my children was making me very depressed. In fact, I was suicidal. I had my suicide planned to the last detail. The urge to take my life was overwhelming and I often wonder whether the spiritual world was influencing me. I don't know why I did not make the attempt I had so carefully planned, but I definitely had second thoughts. These experiences helped me cope with my depression by arousing my curiosity. They went on for about two years: hardly a night went by without me experiencing some type of out-of-body state. The Eckankar people told me how to bring on such a state by using a certain chant. I tried it and, amazingly, I could lift out of my body at will.

Later, during a holiday back in Melbourne, I visited a New Age bookshop and bought a book on astral projection. I wanted to learn so much more, because I wanted that feeling of peace again. I needed to know what was happening to my mind and body and, even though the book was incredibly lengthy, I couldn't put it down. Everything that had happened to me was actually there in the book in case histories—vibrations, paralysis, face contortion, floating, bells ringing, water falling, and 'explosions' occurring in the head. One night I even heard beautiful, mystical music. I couldn't wait for more to happen and went to bed with great anticipation, hoping that a technique I had read about would induce a different spiritual experience.

Nothing happened the first night and I was disappointed. The second night as I lay in the foetal position, still conscious enough to hear the clock ticking, I felt my body begin to vibrate and become paralysed. Then my whole body, including my face, began to contort. I couldn't move; all I could do was groan. My neck twisted back, my body arched, yet something appeared to be trying to get out of my throat. A male voice was telling me to turn over, so I kept trying until eventually I managed to move. In spite of my panic, I was aware that only my spirit body had turned over—physically I hadn't moved. I was still in the foetal position when, thankfully, the whole experience stopped. I was so terrified I dropped any further experimentation and returned to Canberra. I didn't want anything more to do with spirits or out-of-body experiences and I desperately wanted return to my normal lifestyle because I really believed I had a devil in me. I was becoming possessed by an evil spirit.

Within a few weeks, in spite of my reluctance, I experienced my first 'physical' spiritual contact. One night in bed I felt 'fingers' scraping down my spine. It was so powerful it hurt and brought on a tingling feeling. It paralysed me, yet I had sufficient presence to mentally ask for it to be repeated. Three times it was repeated: I wanted to be convinced that it was a spiritual force and not my imagination. Again, I wondered whether it was evil because that same night I felt 'fingers' being inserted into my vagina. I recall being aroused, but when I realised what was happening, I told them to 'fucking piss off'! I didn't want my physical privacy intruded upon by a 'randy spirit'. In spite of my trying to avoid the experience during the next few weeks I was still occasionally tapped on the shoulders and I would hear a voice saying 'Liz'.

I had begun to find these events so terrifying that I didn't want anything more to do with the darker side of spirits. As it turned out, nothing much happened for about nine years and then the experiences returned with a vengeance ... in brothels! Why I don't know, but over those years I had come to miss the intense excitement they caused, so by the time I became a sex worker I was well and truly ready for more.

Ghostly antics in brothels
3

My introduction to ghostly activities in a Canberra brothel occurred in 1992. A girlfriend said to me, 'Strange things have been happening, you've got to come over!' I loved the idea of 'a make-up bag being thrown across the room by an unknown force' and I couldn't wait to see if it was true.

Sure enough, it wasn't long after I started work at the brothel that I also experienced unexplained happenings. Another hooker and I witnessed a large fern rattling in a plant holder. She appeared absolutely terrified and, although I was a little shaken, I wondered whether she might somehow have contrived the incident. From then on I watched her like a hawk, but it was hard to be sceptical because when we walked around the studio small objects such as pencils often dropped at our feet; occasionally an object was thrown with great force. Then larger things started getting thrown around—shoes, a knife and spoon, a candle holder. In retrospect, it seemed that the 'happenings' were a deliberate attempt to catch my attention. For example, a group of us were sitting in the reception area when a sweet was thrown at our feet—which set off an intriguing series of events.

All the windows and doors were locked, as is the usual practice in a brothel, so how the sweet was thrown inside was a mystery, even more so after we heard a knock at the back door. When we opened the door we were confronted with bars of chocolate lying on the ground. Even more mystifying, there was an open packet of sweets of the same brand as the sweet thrown inside the brothel! We were suspicious and nervous, so we threw the chocolates and the sweets into the rubbish bin outside the brothel. When we walked back inside, the telephone rang and when we answered it an odd, high-pitched voice whispered 'Did you like the lollies?' Within minutes we received another call, this time a deep, gravelly voice saying, 'I'll see you on the other side.'

It was all very strange but, although I was scared, I loved what was happening and spoke to the spirits to encourage them. To be honest, at the time I thought the telephone calls were probably from a crank and that I was being duped. But as I look back now I'm not so sure: so many things that I can't explain have happened to me.

Of all people, I ended up telling my psychiatrist about the unusual activities I seemed to have been attracting, but as usual he was little help. All he wanted to do was prescribe lithium carbonate, a drug commonly used for schizophrenic patients, and to document the information for inclusion in his file.

I did not stay at that brothel for long, but I somehow missed the strange activities and felt disappointed that I would never again witness such things. How wrong I was!

I began working at another brothel in Fyshwick, and this marked the beginning of my journey into the spirit world. It wasn't long before I was labelled 'the ghost lady'. Some of the girls were excited about my activities; others were very scared. Some wanted to work only on my shifts, to watch the action; others refused to share my shifts. Management was not at all happy. I soon developed such a rapport with the spirits that, in the presence of other girls, I could summon the spirits to phone the brothel. Yet no one ever spoke when other girls answered. I also developed the ability to ask, and get, the spirits to throw objects (usually the girls' cosmetics) in front of fellow prostitutes.

News spreads quickly in brothels and, with so many tongues wagging, it wasn't surprising that the brothel soon got the reputation of being haunted. It was rumoured it was haunted before I even went there: I was told the activity started many years earlier, after an excited client found it all too much and suffered a fatal heart attack 'on the job'. It was said that the staff carried him out of the brothel, put him in his car, and drove the car down the street. This was years ago, when prostitution was illegal and nobody wanted the complications caused by a dead body on the premises.

Few were surprised when management decided to get rid of me. Owners are not known for their benevolence. Girls were leaving because they were frightened of me, but above all management thought I was affecting the profits. On the other hand, they knew I was an excellent worker and after friends intervened the decision was reversed—on the condition that I behave. But they got rid of me again after two of us went to a Canberra television station.

I had heard that management was seeking the services of an exorcist from Goulburn and I wanted to stop it by having cameramen and reporters interfere with the exorcism. I didn't want my spirit friends to go. In truth, we didn't know whether an exorcism was going to take place or whether the bosses simply set up a rumour to make the girls believe the ghosts were gone. I don't know to this day whether an exorcism took place. The television station knew it was a good story, but as soon as the boss heard about the media's interest I was sacked. Powerful businessmen run brothels and they don't want people believing the brothels are haunted: the publicity could ruin them.

After all the drama died down business was very quiet, so I was re-employed there. Business did pick up, but my spirit friends renewed their antics: rubbers, pens, coasters—anything light and moveable—were thrown. Flowers were pushed off the tables in the long, dark hallway. The telephone would ring once when I entered the brothel to start my shift, and I knew it was my spirits' way of acknowledging me. Often I was touched on the head or shoulders; other girls also felt this invisible hand.

But this wasn't all that I experienced: I felt a 'power of love' when I entered the brothel, which at times was so overwhelming that I was taken aback. I knew this 'thing' loved me, but I still didn't know what it was. I tried speaking to spiritualists in Sydney and locally. They said. 'It must go to the light'—meaning to be moved from its earthbound state—and I thought, 'Bullshit, it's not going anywhere!' I loved my spirits, I didn't want them pissing off. By now I felt no fear, only excitement, and I couldn't resist the temptation to explore further.

Several months passed before I decided to investigate, through other sources, what was happening. I contacted another spiritualist group in Sydney and told the 'ghost buster' the chain of events surrounding my contact with the spirits. She warned me about the possible dangers associated with my delving. I didn't take much notice. Later, I contacted a member of the Spiritualist Church in Canberra and she advised me to contact Canberra clairvoyant Monica Hamers. I didn't confine myself to spiritualists: I also contacted the Australian Skeptics in Melbourne and was given the name of a professor at the Australian National University to see if he would be interested in investigating my case. I spoke to the professor and told him that I had an appointment with Monica

Hamers. He claimed someone he knew had 'set up' Monica, but ironically found her to be genuine and very accurate. Personally, I was doubtful about clairvoyance, but very curious.

When I visited Monica she put me into a trance. I have never been a good subject for hypnosis: it was often used in the treatment of my earlier medical problems. During the trance Monica asked me to picture a particular scene, and I tried hard to relax but found it difficult. Monica asked me, among other things, what I was seeing. I replied, 'A shepherd' because a picture of a shepherd was dominating my mind. Although it meant nothing at the time, later the vision started to make sense. At the end of the reading Monica told me to leave a lipstick in front of the mirror in my room at the brothel and ask the spirit to 'write his name'.

That night I was on late shift but I decided not to tell anyone about my visit to Monica. It was with great anticipation that I went into my bedroom, not really expecting any results because it all seemed so far-fetched. Hookers don't go into other hookers' rooms but I wasn't taking any chances and I watched everyone very closely.

Within a couple of hours I was shaking with excitement: there, in the corner of the mirror, written with the lipstick I had left, was a shaky heart with an arrow through it. Alongside the heart were the words 'I love you Liz'. But I was ecstatic when they wrote on the mirror later that night, 'Dear Liz, I have been trying to contact you. I have been with you. I was with the shepherd you saw on the hill. I have to go now or I will die. I will contact you again. Love, Matt.' I was over the moon; real contact at last! With whom or what I didn't know and at that moment I didn't really care.

It wasn't long before the 'force' started becoming more powerful. Artificial palm trees were shaken vigorously and one of the tallest ones, about two metres high, was hurled down the hallway. None of the girls had the strength to throw that tree with such force. Of course, we blamed each other for playing tricks, but none of the girls would walk around the brothel on their own if I was on their shift. I walked out of the brothel kitchen one night and saw a baseball bat just lift out of a plant holder and be thrown hard against the wall. It was a genuine wooden baseball bat and I don't know to this day if it was in the brothel for protection or if it had manifested from somewhere else, but we never found it after that night.

As if to reassure me, words were written on my mirror—'Don't worry about Ben; he won't hurt you'—but I was beginning to wonder. Once when I was 'playing' with the spirits I held a lipstick to the mirror to see if they could move my hand to write. I became frustrated when nothing happened and walked to the kitchen, where I vented my disappointment on the bemused receptionist. Next minute, a large, heavy, mattress that was on the floor in the kitchen flew up and hit me in the face, knocking me over. I was shaken because I hadn't seen it coming. The receptionist, who had been sitting in the far corner of the kitchen, was horrified to see the mattress knock me down.

The 'force' was able to do an amazing variety of things—it even threw ice down my jumper. I loved pushing it, to see how far I could go. But one day I went way over the top, causing the spirits to become intensely angry about something only I knew I had done. The power of what I had created and then abused really terrified me.

Liz never told me what it was she had done.

Within days things came to a head. I heard loud banging on the walls when I entered the brothel to start my shift. I assumed the spirits were doing this to let me know that they were upset, so I was very reluctant to stay on my own. I walked with the receptionist down to the end of the hallway, where our attention focused on the loud ticking of a clock. As we turned and looked into one of the bedrooms a vase full of plastic flowers was thrown from behind us with incredible force. For the first time I was petrified: I knew I had really upset the spirits. Panicking, I ran into the bedroom where I worked and yelled to the spirits, 'What's wrong? What have I done? Please tell me.' Quickly I put a lipstick in front on the mirror, hoping that maybe I could be reassured that everything was okay. I returned to the hallway, where five other girls and one gay prostitute were gossiping, oblivious of my concern. I, on the other hand, fretted, anxiously waiting for a reassuring message. There seemed to be a long, awful calm and then—wham! The gay prostitute, who was holding a bottle of window cleaner, was thrust up against the wall in the hallway by an invisible force, and a bouquet of artificial flowers was hurled towards his body. The window cleaner was ripped out of his hands, causing one of his fingers to bleed. I screamed in fear: this spirit meant business. We were all in a panic, which was made worse when the gay yelled out, 'It's trying to get inside my body.' He pointed at me and screamed, 'Get her out of here, she's evil!'

I knew he was right—I was the cause. I ran to the girls' room and pleaded to a 'sex-change' who I knew had an interest in spirits, 'Help us, we need an exorcist. Something terrible is happening.' 'She' tried to calm me, saying, 'Settle down. You'll only upset them more if you call an exorcist.' Her assurance didn't help and I ran back to the gay guy— but he wasn't there. Then all the lights went out. I was nearly insane with worry. I yelled at the gay to answer us. We were all terrified because we thought he had been taken. Eventually the lights came on and we found him in a bedroom huddled in the foetal position against the end of the bed. His body was rigid, his skin clammy and white. Even though we were still scared we tried to reassure him, and I begged him to accept that I wasn't evil. Eventually he calmed down.

Thoroughly shaken, I returned to my bedroom. There, written in lipstick on the mirror, were the words, 'Now I lay myself down to sleep and I hope that my friends let me rest. I have spoken to the other ghosts and they have to sleep too, and if you don't terrible things can happen. Take this as a warning.' I was so frightened I swore I would never enter a brothel again. The girls, still terrified, wanted reassurance and called the police. Of course, that was a stupid thing to do because the cops simply made jokes about ghosts. And, of course, they couldn't find anyone.

Eventually I returned to work, very chastened by the incident and determined I wouldn't encourage the spirits again—even though I missed the excitement. Ironically, the gay guy became increasingly interested in the spirits. He was virtually a stranger to me and, like anybody working in the sex business, my private life had been kept secret. But he was able to tell me not only my children's first names but their middle names, the contents of my garden shed (which included a broken windscreen that had fallen down and smashed only the day before), the names of my direct relatives who were still alive, and even about my ex-husband's sexual habits. Only I knew that detail. It was uncanny.

Life returned to normal—more or less—except when a couple of cops paid for a 'double'. Cops are regular clients and this night the spirits were rampant, causing the pair to complain about the disruption in the bedroom. Massage oil, tissue boxes and other objects were constantly being thrown around the room and the cops really believed the other girl and I were creating the disturbances to upset them. How they maintained their erections with all the activity going on was a marvel to us. We had a good giggle afterwards, but the cops were not happy and left grumbling that we were the most stupid whores they had ever been with.

In spite of their malevolence, the spirits eventually became my 'servants' and, within reasonable limits, I could usually get what I asked for, whether it was to find my tweezers or a shoelace. Following my verbal request, the object would simply 'appear' at my feet. I once asked for a $5000 cheque I had written out and lost: moments later the cheque simply landed in front of me.

To the average person, Liz's 'ability' may seem impossible. I thought so until I was present during a night of intense poltergeist activity. I asked Liz for a torch to collect an object that had rolled under the bed. She didn't have one. A pocket torch appeared near my hand, 'from thin air' within seconds. Unbelievable maybe, but true.

The phone became an integral part of my communication with the spirits. An interesting example occurred one late shift, in the presence of the receptionist and another girl. When the phone rang and the receptionist answered 'someone' would immediately hang up. After several calls, the frustrated receptionist turned to me and said, 'You answer it.' The voice responded in a stilted manner, 'Play with me' and then hung up. I was beside myself with excitement and yelled out, 'Tell me why you love me, spirits.' The phone rang again and I picked up the receiver: 'We love you, Elizabeth. You are the only true believer.' This was followed by a repulsive laugh. The voice was deep and distorted, and it appeared to require great effort for the 'speaker' to force the words out, yet it was clear enough to understand. We turned the television and heater off so I could hear more clearly and within minutes the phone rang again. Curiosity got the better of another girl but as soon as she picked up the receiver the line went dead. The phone rang again and I answered. This time I heard the words of a woman saying in an extremely high pitched voice, 'It's freezing cold in here.'

Again the phone rang, and I became annoyed when I couldn't understand the voice. Just the slightest noise was enough to muffle the words. The receptionist, another prostitute and I talked excitedly for hours about the calls. It was amazing: in the end I would yell out, 'Ring on the phone again, spirits' and the phone would ring. We'd run up to the office and answer it but unfortunately on the later calls all we could hear was a continual high-pitched tone.

Besides the phone contact, I had an interesting experience during an escort job, which seemed to suggest that 'contact' was from an intelligent source. A friend was driving me to the job, at a city motel. I was running late and had accidentally locked the front door and left the keys in the house, along with her cigarettes. We were both irritated because it was too late to try and break in. As we were driving along I said, 'Wouldn't you love a smoke now?' (I always found cigarettes a source of comfort and I was nervous about fucking a stranger at a motel.) Much to our surprise, and delight, within seconds of making that comment a packet containing six smokes landed on my knees, 'thrown' from the back of the car, it seemed. We couldn't believe it! To top it off, when we returned home, my front door was unlocked and the keys were sitting on the bench where I had left them.

Masturbation to prostitution

Liz's first sexual experiences took place in a bath when she was five. She and her brother used to play a game of making it go hard then soft again. 'I was fascinated by this magic,' she recalled. 'I'd rub his penis but I wouldn't let him touch me—even at that age I liked to be in control.'

> Inevitably, Mum caught us. He was lying down and I was rubbing his dick and that was the end of our baths together. I was about the same age when I said to Mum, 'What does fuck mean?' She went berserk, yelling at me, 'Don't you ever say that terrible word again.' And I thought, 'Was it really that bad?' So I said again innocently, 'But what *does* fuck mean?' This time she became absolutely manic. All I wanted was an explanation that would satisfy a young child, but her reaction scared me. Mum told me it was the worst word in the world. I later found out she was wrong—it was the best!
>
> I was always an inquiring child and by the time I reached eight or nine I was looking through the keyhole of my brother's bedroom door, watching him dry himself off, and,

when I had the chance, watching my father undress too. I really didn't know why I had this interest in naked bodies, but I always enjoyed the pleasure a body could give, even though I didn't realise it was sexual. But my introduction to sexual pleasure came courtesy of an animal. I used this later in life, when I wanted to turn guys on, especially the kinky ones. Their ears would prick up when I asked them if they'd heard the story of Rin Tin Tin. Most knew Rin Tin Tin was a German shepherd, and then I'd tell them about my first orgasm—not through a German shepherd; rather, the family border collie.

I was only about nine and bored with watching television. So I began touching myself and encouraging the dog to sniff and lick my fingers. I ended up with my legs wide apart, one foot on the mantle piece and the other flung across the armchair, letting the dog in for a closer inspection. The dog seemed to enjoy licking me, and I was more than happy for him to continue. I had no idea what a cunt was used for, apart from urinating, but suddenly I started to have this really powerful sensation, the most wonderful thing I had ever experienced. I had no idea what it was but once I'd started that was it—I was hooked. I took every opportunity to be alone with my dog. He really got into the action; he even knew when I was coming because he would lick even faster. I loved it and he loved it.

Looking back, I must have been adventurous even then: here I was, a pre-pubescent girl trying every position. Sometimes I was on all fours in front of the mirror so I could watch the dog behind me. I was so intrigued by this newly discovered pleasure that I found myself sitting in front of the mirror with the dog between my legs, trying to find out where these incredible sensations were coming from. My parents became suspicious because I was always taking the dog into the bedroom. Mum would yell out and ask what was I doing and I always replied angrily, 'My exercises, what do you think?'

When a guy first went down on me, when I was 19, I thought, 'Jesus, my dog did that!' I remember when my first husband fucked me I didn't really see any point in it, but I loved him going down on me because of the memories. I could only reach orgasm if I fantasised about my earlier experiences with the border collie. I probably decided to marry my second husband because he knew how to use his tongue. But no man has matched the intense orgasms I achieved with my collie!

I thought my experiences with my dog were going to remain a deep, dark secret, but recently I had a surprise during a drinking session with a fellow hooker at a Canberra tavern. Like anyone who shares the same profession, we were talking work, having a good laugh as we exchanged stories about our escapades with clients. After a few Scotches, we lost our inhibitions and I told her I'd had sex with a dog. She was in stitches and said, 'Did he fuck you?' I replied, 'No, but I would have let him if he'd known how!' Customers were staring at us because we were laughing so much the tears were pouring down our cheeks. If only they knew.

We were like two schoolgirls exchanging intimate secrets. And then she dropped her bombshell—her best orgasms were courtesy of her pet rat Phantom. I asked her how a rat could lick your cunt. Breathlessly she replied, 'He didn't. He used his claws and gnawed on my clit, and he used to get right into it as though he knew exactly what he was doing.' He loved it, she said, and when Phantom died she was devastated: 'Where would I ever find another rat like Phantom?' It was just as well we were pissed, but we both agreed that no man could reach the standards set by my collie and her Phantom!

My dog was not the only animal I've enjoyed sex with. I often took the family cat, a gorgeous Chinchilla, to bed with me. It wasn't long before she got the taste for it, but her tongue was very rough, to the point where it hurt, and sometimes she bit me on my clit. That immediately destroyed any chance of orgasm. The cat's name was Caressa, and my girlfriend and I would joke that Caressa Clitoris might be a suitable name to use if we ever showed the cat publicly. She was a beautiful cat and I loved her name, so I eventually decided to use it for my own professional purposes.

Later, in my teens, I got my kicks from riding horses, rubbing myself against the pommel of the saddle. I knew then why so many teenage girls love their horses—it was their first introduction to sexual pleasure. I also experimented with other ways of achieving orgasm, including sitting in the bath with my feet above the taps when the shower hose was attached. The pressure of the water on my clit was sensational and I could adjust the intensity of the orgasm by altering the force of the water. That method became a little embarrassing: Mum was cleaning the bath one day and yelled out to me, 'How did footprints get on the walls?' Sure enough, there was a clearly defined set of footprints, and I thought, 'Christ, how will I ever explain that one?' But I could always cover my arse when it came to excuses and, like a trusting mother, Mum always believed me ... or did she? I have never been game to ask.

Part of my sexual education came through an older woman who confided to me that she masturbated. Naturally, I was curious. I asked her how she did it? She went to great lengths to explain to me what an orgasm felt like, and I wondered if that was the thing I was feeling. She used a pig-bristle hair brush, so I rushed out and bought one. I experimented with both ends, but found the handle more satisfying. I still have that 'old faithful' 22 years later, although it's a bit worn now. I will never throw it away. It 'comes' with me everywhere!

Although I engaged in heavy petting and oral sex, apart from my youthful 'cemetery sex', I didn't have sexual intercourse until I met my husband. The marriage disintegrated quickly but at no stage did I consider prostitution. I was faithful to my husband: I teased the life out of other guys, but I never screwed them. I flaunted myself because I wanted them to take notice of me.

When I finally left my husband I was a psychological mess and needed something to take away the pain caused by the broken marriage. I wanted an instant fix and decided a car was the solution. Initially, all I wanted was a cheap $400 car. But, as is typical with me, I suddenly decided that wasn't good enough and I wanted a red MGB. I wanted it now, no matter what. I was unable to get a loan from the bank, so I rang Mum: 'If you don't lend me the money for the car, I'll become a prostitute.' I was so naive I didn't even know prostitutes existed in Canberra; I thought they were all Kings Cross heroin addicts.

Mind you, the MG became a secondary issue after I talked to a girlfriend in the Public Service who admitted making great money as a hooker in Bali. The idea really excited me. She was gorgeous, absolutely beautiful. She told me I could also make big money. Wow—my problems would be solved. There was a moment's hesitation, when I wondered how could I take my clothes off in front of a total stranger, but it didn't last long.

The following day I rang the manager of a Fyshwick brothel and she invited me to meet the girls that night. I was burning with curiosity. I wanted to see what a real prostitute looked like and when I arrived it was just how I had imagined. The place was dark and sleazy, with the smell of sex in the air. A fat, bottle-blonde hooker who was sitting in the corner gorging Chinese food treated me like shit, yet I was talked into starting that night. The girls criticised my appearance and tried to pack heavy make-up on my face and adjust my clothing. I thought, 'No way am I going to look like a tart' and buttoned up my dress in disgust. No way was I going to flash my tits.

Soon I came upon a wall of silence: I had no idea how much the girls disliked being questioned. When I asked a couple of them how long they had been prostitutes they wanted to attack me and threatened the receptionist that if I continued to work with them they would walk out. How was I to know they didn't like being called prostitutes? I asked other girls what it was like working in a brothel and once again I was verbally abused. They insisted it was a 'parlour'. According to them, that was a much nicer name, but as far as I was concerned they were sluts working in a whorehouse.

The boss told me I was 'too old' to work in the brothel—men liked 18-year-olds—so she decided to use me as an escort. I looked at one fat, ugly slut and said to the receptionist, 'Jesus Christ, don't the guys want a little bit of class compared to that?' I asked the boss if I could have a drink of wine. My nerves were shot to pieces as I tried to come to grips with the fact that I was a prostitute and about to sell my body. She refused, although she had no hesitation in offering other girls marijuana. Another girl had started that night and was totally off her face, on what appeared to be heroin. She couldn't even walk straight, yet was accepted by the other girls. I didn't understand why I was ostracised.

My introduction to prostitution was not what I expected. The manager walked me to the motel and explained to the client that it was my 'first time' and to be gentle with me. The guy didn't want to fuck me because I was brand new in the game. He was a genuinely nice person and tried to talk me out of prostitution and to go away with him. I wasn't interested: I had only just started and I was curious to see what it felt like to fuck a stranger and get paid for it. It seemed so easy. It was a case of 'give me your money for nothing' and I quickly became comfortable with the idea of receiving large amounts of money for very little effort.

I had a second client that night and when I went to his flat

I genuinely had no idea what to do. I had no training—all the manager had told me was to check his cock for diseases. I could barely look at his cock, let alone ask him for the money. I was so uncomfortable I turned away from him when I took my clothes off. He wanted me to suck his cock and he came in my mouth. Thank God he asked me if I wanted to spit it down the sink. I thought I might have embarrassed him if I'd asked to spit it out. (In those days you got the sack if you used condoms—you only used them if you suspected the client had a disease.) The experience was so clinical I wondered if I could continue. In the end I worked only two nights at that brothel: I couldn't stand the way I was being treated by the other girls. They were hard-core whores and at the time I believed I was too good to work with rubbish like that!

I returned to the Public Service but it was no use. I had developed a taste for the large amounts of money I could earn, and the freedom. So I soon began working for another brothel, in Weston. Ironically, for that supposed mental freedom I paid a heavy price in my early months of prostitution. In one hectic period I attempted to earn $40 000 in three months. I wanted to get my MG restored and get rich. I was also vulnerable and naïve: I thought I could get away with taking Duromine (an amphetamine) to stay awake and Mogodon (a sedative) to go to sleep. Finally, I cracked up from mental and physical exhaustion and was admitted to hospital for six weeks. My ambition to get rich had failed. I was very vulnerable after leaving hospital and I was courting disaster.

I met a guy at the Private Bin, a popular Canberra nightclub. He was very desirable and appealed to me romantically, but when I told him I didn't want to go home with him he just turned away to talk to other girls. My confidence was at rock bottom, and I was really hurt that all he wanted was a fuck. I was also deeply depressed by being on my own on New Year's Day, so I went back to

Gowrie Private Hotel, where I was living, bought a packet of cigarettes and swallowed all the medication I could get my hands on. I was found in a state of total confusion and taken to hospital to have my stomach pumped out. I slept for a week.

While I was recovering an elderly Roman Catholic priest, in whom I put my trust, came to visit me. As he spoke to me he grabbed my hand and put in on his robe. He held my hand so close to him I know I felt a hard-on and I thought to myself, 'Holy shit! It couldn't be, not at his age. A priest wouldn't be like that.' But I admit I left my hand there. He knew I was a prostitute and visited me twice a day. He made me feel so uncomfortable: I had always put priests on a pedestal. I tried to believe it was something else—a torch or something—in his robe, but I knew it was his cock. After I left hospital the priest followed up my recovery and was always waiting for me in the Gowrie foyer. I tried everything to avoid him but what upset me most was that he had visited my mother. He told her I was a prostitute but said he was prepared to leave the priesthood because he was in love with me! Mum was horrified and ordered him out of the house.

Unfortunately, we met again accidentally and I agreed to have a coffee with him in Kingston. As we were walking along the pavement, I was disgusted to see him pick up a dirty old comb and put it in his pocket, saying, 'It might come in handy.' While drinking coffee, he told me he had worked in the country and had been accused of molesting Aboriginal children. Apparently, he used to sit the kids on his knees, to let them steer the car while they went for a drive. I asked him if he had really done it and he replied, 'Of course not.' I remember a gay nurse I knew from Canberra Hospital repeating one of his sick jokes: 'What's better than a 12-year-old boy? A 6-year-old boy!'

After I left hospital I knew I would never go back to the Public Service. It was much easier to lie on my back being a prostitute than to sit over a typewriter thinking about my constant obsession—food. In many ways, prostitution was a wonderful escape because all my life I suffered emotional stress, primarily because of my desire to be slim and beautiful. This pursuit of beauty caused severe bulimic and anorexic disturbances, which wasted 14 years of my life. It also crept into my work life: I was a first-class secretary, yet my life revolved around hanging my head in a toilet bowl and I often was absent from work because of my preoccupation with food. In contrast, with prostitution I could work when I wanted to and vomit when I wanted to.

* * *

I'm proud of what I do. There's a reason God created hookers. I'm one of God's children and I know He looks after me. The Catholic Church says no to prostitution, but I say that's bullshit. My destiny has been set out for me and it's God's way of telling us that prostitutes provide a valuable service to the community. I can help men with their problems and their loneliness. I'm especially here for the men who are perverted and kinky, so they don't impose their will on innocent women or children. With prostitution, I have my own freedom, plenty of money, and the chance to work without any pressure from bosses wanting to know where I've been or why I haven't been sitting at my desk. In fact, I get more respect from my clients than I did from my former professional bosses.

Prostitution has saved my life in many ways. I've had the money to change my body, to alter what I didn't like. I receive plenty of attention from men who desire me, and this has given me the confidence to be proud of myself and what I am. The mental freedom that came—when I no longer had to sit on a chair in front of a typewriter with a bunch of bitching girls who were continually eating—was sheer bliss!

In my next life I want to come back as the world's best

porn star. I've never starred in a porn movie but I'm an exhibitionist when it comes to sex. I'll do most things as long as I'm paid. I've had three men at once—vaginally, anally and orally—and indulged in raunchy group sex. I've even been raffled off. Ironically, my greatest fantasy before I became a prostitute was to have sex with another woman, but when an 18-year-old girl finally went down on me I was disappointed. My first real lesbian encounter was with a 55-year-old American woman I worked with. She drove me home one night in her Trans Am and asked me what I thought of cunnilingus. I thought, 'Shit, this is heavy.' I could hardly talk. She had brought me presents at work and now I know why. She touched me, saying, 'I feel more for you than you would ever believe.' When I arrived home that night I flogged myself like hell because it really turned me on that a 55-year-old woman had the hots for me.

I must emphasise that some activities I describe here are quite disturbing. Yet, just think about the number of rapes and perverted attacks I have prevented. My telephone rings 24 hours a day, with men asking to have their fantasies, perversions and fetishes fulfilled. Prostitution will always be around and should be legalised everywhere: that way it is kept under some sort of control and away from major crime.

Australia now has its first brothel for women. Do men feel threatened now that women have access to an establishment that caters for emotion-free, unadulterated sexual pleasure? The Boardroom of Melbourne opened for business in May 1997, starting with more than 15 men on its books. Women of all types have taken the plunge. And, as one 'service provider' (the term used for the Boardroom prostitutes) commented, 'Most of the women I see are very normal. You'd see them in the office or in the supermarket; they just want to relieve some stress and have a good time without the emotional ties. Why not? Men have been doing it for centuries.'

Another worker reflected Liz's comments on why men seek

prostitutes: 'There are a lot of lonely women out there.' Yet, he continued, 'Women are as much into fantasy as men. A lot of women like to be tied up or want me to dress in leather. Sometimes two female friends want me to join them for a threesome. Others want me to talk dirty or masturbate them. Some just want company and affection without sex.'

It could be Liz talking about her male clients. Might this be the start of real emancipation for women? I wonder how the acid tongue of *The Female Eunuch*'s author, Germaine Greer, would describe this new establishment? Or, indeed, would she have taken advantage of such a facility in her youth?

Interestingly, and on a more practical level, the five-star establishment comes at a cost. Women are expected to cough up a minimum of $120 for half an hour and about $200 for an hour. Although one has to admire the designer's attention to detail: even the mattresses are a special compressed foam, as opposed to the normal spring mattress, to avoid back injuries during vigorous activity. Finally, The Boardroom gives unisex another meaning. It also provides female prostitutes for men and the growing number of women with lesbian fantasies. We now have holistic medical centres where you can have treatments from herbalists to traditional practitioners. Why not brothels to cater for both sexes?

If you feel intimidated about using brothels—male or female— what about using the services of a surrogate? Most young men dream of meeting an older, more experienced woman who not only enjoys passionate sex but can also teach the novice sufficient sexual etiquette to ensure that the most timid girl's knicker elastic will melt in the face of his charms. On the other hand, most young girls dream of succumbing to appropriate wooing and finally love. My experience suggests that this idealised, romantic approach to sex changes with maturity and increasing emancipation. The older, more sexually confident woman expects, and indeed demands a male with not only sensitivity but also a reliable libido. The ageing man looks back with envy at his youth, when masturbating three times a day was essential to keep his mind on studies and sporting pursuits. Now balding and overweight, he wants to divert the woman's attention from his lack of bedtime performance with excuses of exhaustion from work (probably true) or a headache from a business lunch (enjoyed to keep away reality).

So did nature get it wrong? There is a grain of truth in my simplistic scenario. The reality is that as men move into their mature years their libido appears to drop, whereas in middle age a woman's confidence and sexual interest are renewed, especially when children become less demanding.

Europe and America have set the trend by using surrogates to assist both men and women with their sexual problems. Legitimate surrogates undergo specialised training before they are let loose on a client. For the observer, this may seem little different from prostitution: sex with a stranger in exchange for money, with the added bonus of a therapist looking on and guiding the training session. One surrogate who worked at the Chelsea Medical Centre in London described the difference: 'One is about buying sex and the other is about acknowledging a problem and being brave enough to find help.'

Liz, however, claims that she has helped numerous men with their sexual problems—from inability to maintain erections to premature ejaculation. Even troubled males in stable relationships have sought her aid. Liz has also provided sex for disabled men who under normal circumstances would be unable to find a partner. In the liberated Netherlands prostitutes are not necessary for this group because sexual helpers are paid to sleep with the disabled. The Dutch authorities pay men and women around $100 a visit to meet the sexual needs of about 350 disabled people in their homes. The organisation is known as the Association for Alternative Relations and on its books are housewives, nurses and psychotherapists who carry out this service. Maybe suitable male and female prostitutes should be trained in the art of therapeutic sexual counselling. Would this bring a legitimacy to a profession that has for so long craved widespread public support?

Surprisingly, Liz is more worried by the consequences of warts, herpes or crabs than HIV. She believes the chance of getting AIDS if a condom slips off or splits is remote. As she says in her normal blunt manner, 'You'd have to be fucking unlucky to catch HIV. Anyway, I must be the only hooker who uses no other contraception than condoms, so I have to be bloody careful. I am very conscious about HIV, and anything that is inserted into me—whether it be fingers, toys or zucchinis—has to have a condom on. So does my vibrator.'

Liz shaves her pubic area daily, to lessen the chances of catching lice, and sprays her bedroom with anti-bacterial agents to reduce the risk of infection. She is terrified of catching a disease, even though she takes all the necessary precautions. She allows anal intercourse with a condom, although she says it took her a long time to learn how to prevent the act being painful.

> 'Clients usually ask on the phone if I do anal, so then I can prepare. Before they arrive, I use gel and insert my own fingers to stretch and relax the sphincter muscles. I only enjoy anal intercourse if I'm in a relationship, rather than getting fucked up the arse with a client and being paid for it. In a relationship, it's extremely erotic. It's not dirty like many people think. I have my own special way of doing it and you certainly don't pull it out with shit all over a client's dick.
>
> I feel I was born for prostitution. I love being a hooker. I tell my clients 'I was born with a silver cock in my mouth' when they ask me why I do it. I know when a man walks out of my bedroom I've made him feel like a man—not only sexually, but as a human being. I love to be responsible for a man's orgasm and for him to receive pleasure from my body. I enjoy sex and frequently have orgasms. Consequently I've earned a lot of money from prostitution because not only do I enjoy sex, I also want to be the best. If I choose to work seven days a week, $7000 is not an unrealistic figure.
>
> Unfortunately, many girls I know are really twisted by the

whole game. They deteriorate rapidly because they take addictive substances so that they can cope with the revulsion they feel. Nothing worries me, but I will not get involved with children. I have initiated youths, but recently a man rang me and asked if I would have sex with a 14-year-old. I replied, 'Bullshit, that's illegal.' He said, 'Don't worry, I won't tell anyone.' I still refused so he rang me back later: 'Well, if you won't have sex with him can he watch the two of us having sex?' I still said no—he was probably a paedophile and the poor, innocent kid his victim.

My personal relationships are invariably with clients or ex-clients because I have a real hang-up about sex outside my work. It's difficult for me to relate to people outside the sex industry and I feel more comfortable once I get the sex problem out of the way and I can work on forming a relationship. I've only screwed one 'outsider' in the last nine years, a guy I brought home from a nightclub. I really liked him but I couldn't see a relationship developing because I felt like a stranger to myself, especially since he didn't know I was a hooker.

Often it doesn't take long for a prostitute to lose her dignity, or her looks. I've seen hookers look shocking after a year. But I've reversed that trend: I've been working for nine years and I look better than ever. Of course, plastic surgery has helped. I've had four facelifts, two nose jobs, three breast uplifts, a tummy tuck, my upper eye lids and lower eye lids lifted, three dermabrasions, and liposuction of my hips, thighs and stomach. I've had frown lines and fatty deposits of skin surgically removed from my face, collagen injections, injectable silicon into facial lines, permanent eyeliner tattooed on upper and lower eyelids twice, lip liner tattooed into my lips twice, and gortex thread inserted in my lips to give them a fuller, more sensual appearance.

I started having plastic surgery at the age of 32 years and, although I have had one scare from an unqualified doctor, I have been a patient of an excellent Sydney plastic surgeon for some years now. It hasn't been really necessary to have some of the facelifts, but the results have been dramatic and I certainly don't look or feel 40 years old. I will continue to have plastic surgery as long as I am able.

Practically the only part of me that's not plastic is my personality, and I don't want that changed. I am very content with the way I am. I consider I am one of the luckiest girls in the world, regardless of my past.'

5
Caressa and her clients

Sex is meant to be a pleasurable interlude and to ensure the continuation of our species. But, for Liz, in her multitude of liaisons with men, women and groups, something she always enjoyed was the funny side of sex. Her first experience was at home.

> I was in my late teens and my mother caught me using a vibrator. The guy I was seeing at the time bought it for me from a sex shop. Mum didn't trust me and often came into my bedroom unannounced to find out what was going on. Well, there I was on my bed with my legs spread wide apart, experimenting with this battery-operated penis and getting close to orgasm. As I was just about to come, Mum opened the door so quietly and I got such a fright that the vibrator flew out of my hand onto the floor. There was this pink cock-shaped thing with a life of its own, shaking away beside my bed. I tried to grab it but it kept moving. I bounced out of bed, my body covering the 'turned-on' penis, and in my most innocent voice asked, 'What's up, Mum?' In retrospect, it probably didn't matter because I

doubt if she had even heard of a vibrator. She finally left the room, none the wiser, ...I think.

When it wasn't my dog or the vibrator giving me pleasure it was one of my early boyfriends, Tony. Occasionally Mum was more diplomatic and, instead of bursting in, she would bang on the door to tell me it was about time Tony 'got out of there'. It didn't always go to plan. I was having a wonderful sixty-niner with Tony and I made sure his head was leaning against the door: that way I could slam the door shut with my foot if Mum came in. Once again, she opened the door very, very quietly. I got a huge fright and flung myself back so quickly that Mum got her fingers jammed in the door and I ended up squashing Tony's face with my arse!

Later, when I became a hooker, there was never a shortage of funny stories to keep us amused during the quiet periods—all of us thrive on gossip. One story I'll never forget involved an impeccably dressed 73-year-old former army major who frequented Northside Studios in Fyshwick. He would walk into the brothel dressed in a freshly pressed suit, complete with long, curled moustache, walking stick, highly polished shoes and an air of authority that convinced us that he was indeed a former army officer. He spoke with a rather pompous voice and always demanded to see the new girls, as though they were recruits to be inspected.

Some of the girls used to look forward to his visits; others dreaded them because the old dear had a technique that would take us to the heights of orgasmic pleasure. Very few men know how to use their tongue, and usually you get advance warning of a man's skill from the way he caresses your nipples with his mouth and tongue. If they get that right they will invariably give good head. The major really knew how to use his tongue! It was an incredible ego trip for the ex-officer to know that at his age he could go down on the young girls and make them come with such intensity. He reasoned that if he brought them to orgasm, they would respond by giving him an even better time.

It was so funny. The girls would emerge from their room after an hour with the major and feel absolutely repulsed because this 'geriatric' they couldn't stand gave them one hell of an orgasm. We deliberately didn't tell the new girls, and we would laugh as they stormed out of their rooms, shouting angrily, 'Jesus Christ, that old bastard just made me come!' They'd complain and ask us why we hadn't warned them. He was also extraordinarily virile: I've been with him when he's had three orgasms in one hour, simply by screwing. Very few men can do that.

You couldn't help but respect the old codger, and we all wondered what he would have been like in his youth. He told me that when he was young he loved oral sex but that not many women 'liked their pussies munched out on in those days' and his wife was disgusted at the thought. Some girls like to stay 'orgasmically faithful' to their regular partners, but with the old major they couldn't help themselves—including me. Maybe I should have introduced him to a lady of 55 I know, who only recently became a hooker. She loves oral sex, particularly from the young blokes. She makes all her clients go down on her because she doesn't get sex, let alone oral sex, from her husband.

I regret it, but in my early days of prostitution I used to drink to enable me to relax with clients. Once, when I was a bit pissed, I swallowed a client's earring. What was worse was that the client was a friend of the brothel's manager and I'd been told to give him a 'special time'. I was trying to make him really horny by gently chewing on his ear, but he had a gold earring in the shape of a cross in his left lobe and it got in the way of my nibbling. No doubt because of my drinking, I hiccupped at the wrong time and swallowed the earring. I tried to disguise my choking with a cough, but really the earring had nowhere to go other than down my throat. After he got his 'rocks off' and relaxed a little he realised his earring was missing. He was angry and accused me of stealing his jewellery. So, we spent the next 20 minutes trying to find his earring in the bedclothes, my hair, and the carpet. I was frightened of this client because he had a reputation for violence, but I also wanted him to think I was the best so he would tell his friends. With all the confidence I could muster I told him not to worry and that I would find his earring. As soon as he had gone I raced home and took a huge dose of Epsom salts. When the earring finally appeared it was a little 'tarnished' and I had to take it to a jeweller to clean it up. The client was none the wiser when I told him I had found it in my hair.

I've always been very good with shy clients because I take my time and listen to them. I've developed a technique to calm their nerves and lower their inhibitions. And occasionally I've offered clients discounts for special reasons. But with one Italian gentleman, who paid me $140 for an hour, even with my special skills I couldn't avoid what ensued. I hadn't even started to undress him and remove my negligee when he asked if he could go to the toilet. I knew he was very nervous and showed him to the bathroom in my most diplomatic manner. He came out looking very sheepish, his head down between his shoulders. I wondered what was wrong and asked him if everything was OK. In a wonderful Italian accent he replied, 'I am sorry Caressa, I have come already.' He was so embarrassed I offered him his money back, but with exemplary Italian chivalry he refused and I never saw him again. It's nice to know that clients get so excited at the thought of making love to you that they ejaculate before you get your knickers off!

I'm often asked if I get embarrassed when I run into clients away from work. Of course, in a small city such as Canberra it's inevitable. One client comes readily to mind because, much to my horror, I later discovered that I knew his partner. He was a cop I screwed at Northside Studios. He booked me for half an hour and I thought, 'Wow, this guy is a really good fuck.' He slid me towards the end of the bed and I put my legs around his neck while he rammed my body back and forth with incredible power. He was highly aroused, with passion written all over his face. Not only was he a good fuck; he was also good-looking and had a great body, which really turned me on. I was having the living daylights fucked out of me and loving it. I said in between his thrusts, 'You're good, really good,' and of course this encouraged him. He was really proud of himself and in reply groaned an obvious 'Am I?' He didn't say much during the session, even during our chat afterwards, which was curious because I find guys in his particular job always like to boast about their exploits.

Later, I was talking with a friend who shares my passion for horses. She was complaining about her boyfriend and how she couldn't put up with him anymore because he was so immature and 'lousy in bed'. The poor girl thought he was having an affair. The way she was talking about him made me feel that the guy was a real bastard. I said to her, 'Fucking leave him. You don't have to put up with that.' She even complained about him spending half an hour in the shower and she didn't know what he was doing. I said, 'I bet I know what he's doing: he's pulling himself.' We laughed.

Some weeks afterwards, I was riding my horse and my friend and her boyfriend, who I hadn't met, were brushing their horse nearby. She yelled out, 'Hi, Liz.' I looked over and caught a glimpse of her partner and thought, 'Christ, I've rooted him!' He had a smirk on his face: he obviously remembered me. During our earlier conversation she had told me her partner's profession and I said, 'I'd love to marry one of them.' She replied dismissively, 'Then you can have him.' Suddenly I recalled that conversation and I really felt like telling her next time, 'I already have, lady, and he was fucking good. I don't know what you're whingeing about!'

A couple of years ago a group of guys from a major sporting institution rang up and said they wanted to play a trick on one of their mates—I think he was a body-builder. They wanted me to pretend I wasn't a hooker but instead a qualified therapeutic masseuse. For the occasion I wore a short skirt, black stockings, and a smart red jacket. I looked more demure than I normally do and when I invited him inside he gave me the envelope, which he believed contained $45 for the half-hour massage. He didn't know there was $85 in the packet and, because he had a leg problem, I don't think he twigged that it was a set-up. My girlfriend was in the room with us, which made the whole exercise appear more authentic. I pretended to him that I was going overseas for two weeks and was just showing my friend the routine for experience, before she took over my 'practice'. He didn't object to another 'therapist' observing. We both acted professionally and I switched on my mood music to help him relax.

I asked him to take off all his clothes except his jocks. Initially, I sat on the side of the bed; then I straddled his body and started my exotic massage. I knew absolutely nothing about therapeutic massage, yet as I dug my fingers into his shoulders he mumbled, 'You can tell I'm a little tight there, can't you?' I replied huskily, 'Yes, just a little stiff. The tension in your muscles needs to be relieved.' He had a magnificent physique and I told him, 'You're so big and in such great shape.' He replied, mumbling again from the pillow, that he did a lot of exercise. I then said, in a sexy voice, 'I bet you're big everywhere!' Well, that was too much for my friend. She got the giggles and did a bolt. Thank God he was on his belly so he couldn't see us laughing.

While I continued rubbing him I managed to take my bra off, so when I finally turned him over all he could see was bare skin and tits. He appeared confused and couldn't work out why, if this was a therapeutic massage, I was semi-naked. But he didn't protest when I started to seduce him. I slowly eased my body down and put a condom on his dick. I've seen thousands of dicks, but I could hardly believe my eyes when I saw this one. It was only an inch long when erect. I wondered whether he might be on steroids: here was this magnificently built man with huge shoulders and monstrous thighs and such a tiny dick. There had to be a problem. All I knew was what the guys who set him up had told me, which was that they had given him some type of protein powder that had a side-effect of making men ejaculate prematurely. They said that although the powder makes men feel really horny and hypes them up sexually, they can't get a proper hard-on. Even so, when he left my place to catch a flight he appeared to be very satisfied. His mates rang back to see how things went. I told them about his one-inch cock and they all had a laugh about that.

Penis, dick, cock, old fella—whatever you like to call it—the male appendage is a source of fascination. A man's ego often revolves around his cock and, no matter what its size or shape, most men believe theirs is not big enough. I've found the length varies from half the length of your little finger to the size of an old school ruler (12 inches). A client in the defence force had one of the most unusually shaped cocks I have ever seen. It had a pronounced downward-shaped, hooked head and because of this I couldn't screw him properly. I had to really manipulate my body to get it in. He always wanted me to give him love bites on his neck, so he could go back to his mates and brag that he'd scored. Another client had a 12-inch long dick that looked like a reverse-shaped boomerang when it was hard. He couldn't screw normally either, so he had to enter me from the back.

It is generally believed the average erect cock is around six inches long. I don't believe that. I've screwed thousands of men and the average is only about four to five-and-a-half inches. The tallest guys invariably have the skinniest and shortest dicks for their size, while men with limited intelligence have the thickest and longest ones. Their average is well over seven inches. God must have granted them big dicks because they don't have much to offer in other ways.

The myth I do want to dispel is about black men. Everyone thinks black guys have the biggest dicks and Asians the smallest. That's bullshit. I remember seeing one black guy around five in the morning at a brothel. I was feeling literally fucked and all I wanted to do was lie in my own bed and sleep. I never fake orgasms, but I thought I would groan a bit to make him think I was enjoying it, which in turn might make him come quicker. While he was thrusting away, he asked, 'Am I hurting you?' I thought, 'Jesus Christ, how could he hurt me with such a small cock'—but he obviously thought he had a big one, even though it was less than five inches long. I've even had clients ring me up and ask me if it's true about black men's penises. There are men who like to brag about their big cocks (or just dream about it) and ring to ask whether I'll be able to accommodate their large penis, because girls they've screwed couldn't take it. You know damn well they're pulling themselves—you can hear it in their breathing—and I tell them jokingly, 'Well if I can accommodate a Shetland pony then I can accommodate you' and hang up!

I've rooted men from many of the world's nations, and their sexual habits and interests vary quite considerably. Asians might not have the biggest dicks, but they are gentlemen, pure gentlemen. The only thing I don't like about some of them is their desire to lick your face and sniff you. They love white women, especially blondes with big tits. One Asian told me that for religious reasons he could not have intercourse with a hooker, so he liked to stick his cock between my legs and root my knees.

Generally, older white Australian-born men are gentlemen, but the young, immature ones are bloody terrible: they often want to prove their manhood by rooting the shit out of you. If they pay for one hour, they want to fuck you for that hour. These types often ask me how many times I will let them come in an hour. I tell them as many times as they are capable. Before they've had an orgasm they're 'full of it', but once they've blown their load they're usually more than satisfied—once is enough! The really virile guys can have four orgasms in an hour but they are exceptions. It is also very rare for a male to have an orgasm and then continue without losing his erection. Females, of course, find it easier to have multiple orgasms, but I have only experienced this through masturbation.

It's not unusual for extremely good-looking 'football-playing macho types' to get together in one room to watch each other screw hookers. Although they do it for kicks, their egos must get shattered because most of them have real trouble maintaining an erection in front of their mates. I have to tell them as casually and diplomatically as I can that it would be easier if the others left the bedroom while I satisfy each one individually. Although they like to treat hookers like shit, they're normally pussycats in these situations and do exactly as I tell them.

Englishmen are usually diplomatic, but I've often found Americans arrogant. One American client I met in a brothel was a real bastard. After we'd agreed on a price and I'd given the money to the receptionist I went back to the bedroom and started my act. I began to suck his cock, but he said he didn't like oral sex and asked me sarcastically what else I could do. When clients have that attitude I get really pissed off: just because you're a hooker you're supposed to know everything about sex, but you certainly don't want to be amorous or adventurous with an arrogant pig. Then he wanted to perform oral sex and make me come but I retorted that I didn't like oral sex either. When he said he'd paid for one hour and he could do anything he wanted to me I became angry. He asked to see the manager. I said, 'Fine, but it's my cunt, not his' and turned round and walked out to the reception area.

The boss wouldn't support me and told me to 'get back in there and give him a good time'. I refused, so he walked down to the bedroom and tried to placate the client. They ended up having a heated argument about who was going to go down on whom. Finally, the manager threw up his hands in disgust and returned the Yank half his money. The manager was pathetic: all he cared about was the reputation of the brothel and the fact that he might have to return some money. One thing brothel management can't handle is parting with the money. They would rather sack a girl than give a refund. I wasn't popular for some time after that incident.

Americans might be arrogant but Italians and Greeks are true gentlemen—the best. They might reek of garlic and body odour but they treat you as a lady. Indians are great, too, although occasionally girls in the industry are extremely rude and call them 'curry munchers'. Turks and Egyptians aren't too bad. They like to exude confidence and might appear dominant and aggressive, but generally they're easy to handle if you know how to manipulate them. The worst are Yugoslavs, particularly Croatian men. They want to fuck the arse off you and when you give them head they either pull your hair or grab hold of your head and force their cock down your throat. I avoid seeing them if I can.

On the other hand, the way some girls treat men in brothels is appalling. I've seen them come out of the bedroom and say, 'The filthy fuckin' old cunt tried to stick his tongue down my throat and then dribbled in my ear' or something like that. A number of hookers are racially prejudiced and refuse to see men of certain ethnic backgrounds, believing they are inferior. I don't really know why: prostitutes have little reason to think they're a cut above anyone else. What does piss me off, regardless of nationality, is the guy who thinks the clitoris is a button you push on and off like a starter motor. It amazes me—when I'm in the 'doggie' position they'll vigorously rub my clit and ask me to come. I have to grit my teeth and groan in pain and at the same time try and direct their fingers elsewhere.

Not all clients are reasonable. I've had my fair share of bastards but I don't accept any bullshit these days. I had a guy on the telephone the other day and he sounded young. I asked him how old he was and he turned the question around by asking how old did I think he was, so I told him 16. He said, 'No, I'm 18.' He asked me if he could fuck me while I stood on my head, so I replied, 'I wouldn't even fuck you lying down.' He then asked, 'Have you got a problem lady?' I said, 'Yes, you sound fucking ugly and you've probably got a little prick.' He called me a whore; I called him a brothel creeper. He said he'd rather fuck his hand than fuck me and I told him to put a condom on it 'so you don't catch warts'! You always know you're going to get a hard time with someone who treats you like that over the telephone.

I can read between the lines and if something sounds amiss, especially when they ask questions like 'How tight's your pussy?' I abruptly end the conversation after a rude comment. One guy phoned me and asked me if I'd lick his arse. He was typical of the male who thinks that just because you're a hooker you'll do anything. Then he asked me how much for 'back-door action' and could he come all over my face. I will do most things for clients, but when it's so blatant on the phone I get very wary. But these men are in the minority—most guys do have respect for hookers.

Some of the activities I get involved in will shock people but, as I said, I believe prostitutes provide a valuable service to the community because they give kinky individuals a legal way of living out their fantasies. One person who comes to mind is 'John the Shitter', who has been around brothels for years. I first came across him when I was working in Weston. In the early days he wanted the girls to dress up in mini-skirts, complete with apron, and no knickers, and walk around the room with a feather duster. Then he wanted us to bend over, insisting that we 'pucker' our arses, and then fart for him. But the thing that most stimulated his bizarre sexual appetite was watching girls shit.

No girl enjoyed the sessions with John, and when he arrived unannounced at the brothel the receptionist would yell out, 'Can anybody shit for John today?' Not all girls were prepared to 'bare their arse' for a price. Those who were willing took Ford pills or other laxatives the previous day, to ensure they could shit for John. The scene was really quite comical if it weren't so sick. The girl would ring John at work and say, 'John, I'm ready. Hurry! I'm nearly shitting myself.' He'd reply excitedly, 'Hold on, don't let go! I'll be over shortly' and he'd rush to the brothel. When he arrived, a toilet, or preferably a bowl, was provided and he would squat religiously beside it and pull himself off as the girl proceeded to live out his fetish. It might surprise some, but he was highly intelligent and, I believe, a professional man, who I'm sure was regarded as totally normal by his friends.

My first experience with John occurred while I was working at Sashas in Fyshwick. It took me years before I was able to bring myself to shit in front of him and I always needed a few drinks to deal with my inhibitions. I charged him $85, plus $50 fantasy money. It should have been easy money for something so natural, but it wasn't. On this occasion, I hadn't taken a laxative but this did not deter John. He liked to try new girls and brought in his own enema to ensure he could be guaranteed a 'motion'. I gather most people can shit after having an enema squirted up their arse, but after

20 minutes or so I still couldn't feel any movement. John became impatient and told me to push. He lay down beside me when I squatted on the toilet, pulling himself off with one hand and with the other holding a torch directly under my arse, waiting for me to shit. We all knew that the harder you shat the more excited he became and the faster he pulled himself off, allowing us to get rid of him quickly and move onto the next client. All I could pass was fluid and John was not impressed. I certainly didn't want to return his money so I was desperate to shit, or at least fart, for him.

We went back to my bedroom to try to work out how I could make him come. I knew I had little chance if I didn't satisfy his fetish. In frustration, he blurted out 'Why can't you fart? You told me you could shit and you can't even fart.' It's not that easy to fart on command, especially when you're under pressure. Then he suggested I lie down while be blew air from his mouth into my arse, but I didn't want him to touch me because I didn't know where his mouth had been. The next best thing was cutting the enema tube in half and letting him blow air through it into my bum. Finally, in one last desperate effort, I threw my legs back, drew them rapidly forward and, thank God, created a reasonably loud fart, which induced John, his right hand moving up and down faster than the pistons on an old steam train, to ejaculate. To him it wasn't a perversion: it was serious business. He preferred to hear loud, strong farts, followed by a rapidly evacuated shit.

I haven't seen John for some years, but I understand he now gets the girls to shit in a bowl and then takes it home, presumably as a catalyst to masturbate. Once he paid me $50 to record myself pissing and shitting on tape—that's all he wanted but it had to be loud and clear. Nothing much embarrasses me, but shitting is pretty personal business. It took me years to fart even in front of my husbands! Few people would suspect John was kinky, although his genitals were malformed: he didn't really have any balls and his dick was small with a huge, ugly head. I still find it amazing how many men don't want contact sex with the girls; they are happy just to pull themselves off whilst watching the girls perform unusual acts.

Most kinky guys are easy to pick. I'm always wary of the ones with the fat arse and belly, protruding eyes, and a beard covering their face. They always seem to have wet lips and their tongue hangs out to one side of their mouth when they're pulling themselves off. Usually they have a foreskin that's never seen soap and water and their personal hygiene is non-existent. Not all kinky clients want the girls to be passive: many are into pain inflicted by the hooker. One client liked me to pinch his nipples as hard as I could, until my finger nails were virtually piercing them. He always brought his own dildo—a type that can't get 'lost' inside you—and his own surgical rubber gloves. What aroused him was to lie down on his back with his legs wide apart and bent towards his head while I gradually eased my glove-covered right hand as far as I could up his arse. He would beg me to push harder, in spite of the fact that his sphincter muscles were squeezing my arm so tightly it hurt. The harder I shoved my arm in and out of his arse the quicker he would climax through masturbation. When he did come, I could feel his whole body powerfully contracting. Occasionally he would screw me normally, but when he was close to orgasm he would always withdraw, pull himself over my breasts, and then lick his own cum.

Another client insisted that I stub cigarettes out all over his erect dick and then pour nail polish remover down the eye of his cock. He hardly flinched. I don't know how he stood the pain, but that's what turned him on. Who am I to judge? I've watched men getting whipped with studded belts until they've bled—and not even cringe. One extremely attractive young businessman wanted B&D [bondage and discipline] and to wear female clothing. A couple of us were curious, so we asked him why he loved being whipped. He told us that when he was a child his mother would lock him in her bedroom cupboard after she had sexually abused and belted him. He said he seemed to gain comfort when he hugged his mother's clothing. Maybe these fetishes do often stem from childhood traumas. I can't bring myself to whip anybody, nor can I be bothered dressing up any more as a schoolgirl or acting the stupid maid. I feel more comfortable with erotic sex.

Some men want you to piss in their mouth 'golden showers'. Others can come only if you wear a pair of knee-length black boots; others love high-heeled shoes that they can lick or rub their dick over; one guy just wanted me to bend over and touch my toes. Most clients who have these fetishes are just happy to masturbate.

Some prominent men in Canberra have very kinky habits. One can only be aroused if he wears plastic baby diapers while the girl wanders about wearing diapers or dressed in plastic. Then he walks around his house, talking business on his mobile phone with one hand and pulling his dick with the other. While one likes plastic, another likes leather. The girls would charge a prominent businessman about $300 an hour and all he wanted was to rub his dick up and down their leather skirts or boots while he masturbated. He enjoyed ejaculating into a glass of wine and then with a great flourish drinking the contents.

Another client used to supply his own special gear so we could dress up. We chose rubber raincoats and balaclavas. He gagged my mouth with a stocking while he wore panty hose with a hole cut out for his dick and his balls. He wanted me to rape him. He said he had seen a psychiatrist about this fetish but was told that as long as he wasn't harming anybody it was okay. Another well-known businessman likes to dress as a woman. He asked me to wear a pink 'baby doll' negligee and wait in the lounge while he prepared himself in his bedroom. When he eventually called me in he was wearing a curly wig and heavy make-up, and had completed the ensemble with bra, high heels, stockings and suspenders. He was an Italian and of course he looked ridiculous, but I had to take the fantasy seriously: a client would be horrified if you laughed at him. What he wanted me to do was lie on the bed and 'adore his beautiful female body', then go down on him like you would a woman. Then he wanted to watch me masturbate with carrots and zucchinis being thrust in and out of my cunt while he pulled himself. If he was not satisfied with these harmless perversions he then involved his German shepherd. The dog appeared accustomed to his owner ejaculating into his mouth and would then enthusiastically lick the cum off his dick.

Group sex can be fun, and I really enjoy threesomes. Not long ago an 18-year-old girl came to my home with her much older boyfriend. He brought along a vibrator with a clit tickler attached. He put it inside her and licked her at the same time. As she was just about to climax he took his mouth away so I could watch her body pulsating, which fascinated me because I had never seen a woman climax at such close quarters. But what really turned the three of us on was the boyfriend and me licking the girl's cunt. It's not unusual for married couples wanting to experience a threesome. In one case I was involved with, the wife had fantasised about the experience for some time and her husband wanted to watch her and another girl while he masturbated and later joined in. Afterwards we shared some wine and talked about the experience. They found it very sensuous and erotic. She was extremely attractive and I felt comfortable fulfilling her sexual needs. I hardly know of a guy who doesn't fantasise about seeing two girls together. But I actually find it incredibly beautiful to see two guys making love.

One of the more outrageous things I've done is 'hooking on the highways'. Some years ago my boss and I were

> operating from Goulburn and Cooma. I must have been crazy, standing in minus eight degrees on the Hume Highway near Goulburn while my friend used her CB radio to hail down the truckies. I was so cold I could barely open my mouth to talk, let alone wrap it around a throbbing dick. There we were, two hookers, jumping into semi-trailer cabs and giving the truck drivers, who were often full of amphetamines, $40 head jobs. There were often queues of drivers waiting patiently for their turn.

Chinese prostitutes had their own version of this. In 1998 about 1000 petrol stations in the province of Ningxia found a way to take service to new heights by offering motorists the delights of a prostitute while their motor vehicles were being topped up!

> In Cooma we would solicit at the local pubs or leave our cards in the men's toilets. It was very risky. Guys would find out where we were staying and bang on our motel doors creating unwelcome attention. If we didn't respond to their requests for a fuck, they'd become aggressive; on one occasion they kicked my boss's car and damaged it. It wasn't surprising when we were finally run out of town, after being thrown out of every motel because word had got around that two hookers were 'bringing the town into disrepute'. Even in the Goulburn *Post* we made front-page headlines: 'Canberra hookers making money out of rich local farmers' or words to that effect. It wasn't the first time I've made headlines: a girlfriend and I once put on a wild show for members of a Yass football club, which created some pious comment in the local media.

> My telephone usually starts to ring at 7.30 am, when most men arrive at work. Ninety per cent of the guys I see are married, in a permanent relationship, or about to be married. They just want something different and, instead of going to a club and picking up a girl, which might interfere with their relationship, they would rather pay a hooker and be free of complications. But some of my clients who see me regularly seek romantic involvement,

which really scares me. I find it much easier to communicate with a stranger than with somebody who wants to have a relationship. Some ask if they can take me away for the weekend, overseas with them, shopping, or to dinner. One bloke in his sixties wanted to take me for a drive down to the coast and I thought, 'Jesus Christ, why do these guys think I'd want to spend a day with them? Do they think I am that bloody desperate and have nothing better to do?'

I guess there are so many lonely older men around and they misinterpret my ability to satisfy them sexually for friendship. Clients often bring me presents such as flowers or chocolates; one always brings me a cake. I had an appointment with a defence force client and he arrived at my home with two lipsticks and an apology because he had to cancel and return to work immediately. The lipsticks were a terrible colour and I wondered if they had belonged to his wife. It was a kind thought, but I would have preferred it if he'd called me to cancel the appointment, so I could 'slip in' another client.

A good hooker can earn a lot of money. On one occasion three of us were hired for an all-night escort at one of Canberra's better hotels. One hooker was not particularly attractive and the guys left her standing in the hallway, while the other girl and I pranced around the bedroom with the wealthy businessmen. After three hours, my friend became ill from drinking too much alcohol, so the men said we could go because they'd had such a good time anyway. The cheque had been written out and signed before we arrived—$5000. Even the old 'school mistress', as we nicknamed her, got paid for standing around doing nothing. Men are very generous when it comes to sex.

You wouldn't expect a judge to use a hooker, but one asked me to visit him at the Pavilion hotel. He was about 40 and absolutely gorgeous. When he told me he was a judge I said, 'I bet you're not a judge, I bet you're on the dole.' He burst out laughing and replied, 'It's as good as being on the dole!' One fellow patient in a Canberra hospital, who later became a client, stole girls' knickers from clothes lines, a habit called 'snowdropping'. He took them home, ejaculated over them, and returned them to the owner's clothes line. He told me he was also a 'sheet rubber': he couldn't come during normal intercourse, so he would rub his dick up and down the sheets of his bed. I've only ever seen this once before, and I found it rather amusing to watch an older man going for broke, head buried in a pillow, madly making love to a sheet!

It's amazing what sets a client off. I had a foreigner recently who arrived at my house with an elastic band already wrapped around his dick. He was difficult to understand, but later I realised he was trying to tell me that he was unable to maintain an erection. The elastic band was tied to the base of his cock so he could insert it inside me. I could barely squeeze it in—it was so soft. Eventually he stuck his cock between my feet, which immediately gave him an erection and he ejaculated all over my toes without a problem.

A few of my clients are pious churchgoers with well-developed perversions. It's as though they have to offset their kinky behaviour with attendance at church. One was a senior member of a local church. The girls in the industry were always curious about this man's position in society. We gave him a very derogatory nickname and he appeared to like the idea of us believing that he was a leading Canberra paramedic, but we never knew the truth. Even the toughest girl could not handle his debauchery: after one hour with him you would find yourself mentally and physically exhausted by the mind games he played. He wanted to talk with you about sex with your mother or animals and would frequently refer to his days in the forces, where he would root the junior sailors. We knew he cruised the brothels to seek out and taunt the new girls. He had to find new victims because most hookers refused to see him.

Another of my regular clients is a professor from the Australian National University. His fetish is 'golden showers' and 'rose leaf' (licking bottoms). He is very experienced and in an hour-long session he can delay orgasm until the last minute. I use 'dental dams' to lick his thighs and balls in case he has any diseases. He loves his nipples being bitten and enjoys my tongue being rubbed up and down his dick, and especially sticking it down the eye of his cock. He normally asks me to perform a sixty-niner and I allow him to lick and put his finger up my arse, as long as I use a dam. He loves arses and usually wants to 'fuck my arse with his tongue', which I let him do for a price. It's all done at a slow pace to ensure he receives maximum pleasure. When he can't control himself any longer, we move to the bathroom and I dim the lights. We both get in the bath, where he gets really turned on by me pissing into his mouth. Finally, what really excites him is watching me piss in spurts over his dick as he masturbates to a climax.

Not all men can handle their guilt following these fantasy trips. Often they become terribly guilty and self-conscious after they have performed sexual acts, acts that they believe society would not normally condone. Society uses qualified psychiatrists or psychologists who have spent many years in training to deal with disturbed patients, yet a prostitute deals with men's twisted sexual activities with no recognition at all. Their only reward is being labelled with less than complimentary names. The partners or wives of people who are into debauchery usually don't know about it, yet many prostitutes are condemned, fined, sometimes jailed, because of their profession. Why should prostitutes suffer while the men who institute this depraved behaviour escape unscathed?

The kinkiest man I've ever met was fat, with protruding

eyes, but he did have a reputation in the brothels for being 'safe', so we didn't mind going to his property because he paid so well. He was really into pain: he enjoyed needles being pierced through his nipples and his balls constricted with a cord until they were purple and nearly bursting. He would provide the needles, cotton, beer bottles, knitting needles, barbed wire or any other equipment he needed to satisfy himself. On my first visit, and with some reluctance, I sewed up his foreskin to the stage where he was unable to piss. His penis actually bled. If I'd had sex with his goats it would have given him even greater pleasure. And the more pain the better, typified by the pleasure he took in his erect, sewn-up cock. We couldn't understand it. He also enjoyed watching two girls piss over him or over each other and vibrators, beer bottles or other items inserted up his arse or our cunts. He always wanted girls who had the hots for each other. He believed we were really full-on lesbians, but we were only acting to take his money. When he had finally had enough we would release his dick so he could pull himself off.

During a further session, another girl and I were at his house for three hours, ending up being paid $900 each. He was very generous and signed an open cheque that we could fill in later. That night we performed lesbian acts, golden and brown showers, Spanish, French and Greek. He enjoyed dressing up in our lingerie: it was laughable watching an obese man becoming progressively aroused wearing a 'teddy'. I was always worried he would have a heart attack and I was even more concerned that I might be responsible for some permanent damage that would allow him to sue me.

He gave me an awful fright one time, when I was at his place alone. He was so aroused that he was completely off the planet and I had to bring him back to reality. I thought he had gone into another world. Even though I was terrified I had sufficient presence of mind to undo all his bondage gear while at the same time trying to pacify him. I thought he could have murdered me because he had totally lost control—although his eyes said he was probably lost in a world of total ecstasy. So much for him being safe. I was alone in the bush outside the city with a man who had lost sexual and emotional control and what appeared to me his sanity.

But the client that really scares me is the one who wants to fantasise about stuff with children. The client who asks me to say, 'Don't, Daddy, don't hurt me.' As a mother of two boys I am very reluctant to take part in these sessions, but at the same time I am aware that I may be saving a child from being molested or raped. People don't realise that prostitutes have real community responsibilities.

I'm constantly surprised at the risks clients are prepared to take, even in this day of HIV. Why clients want to go down on prostitutes, even before they've met them, amazes me. They often ask me over the telephone if they can lick my bottom. I try to deter them by saying that it's risky having oral sex with a prostitute and that if I let everybody go down on me I could catch a disease, then pass it on to another client, who, in turn, could pass it on to their partner. This makes them think twice, but sometimes they say they will take the risk. Before condoms were compulsory, I worked for a while with a junkie who hated men. She thought it was a great joke when guys went down on her: 'Let the filthy bastards lick my cunt if they want to after ten other mugs have just blown inside me.' In those days, the girls moved quickly on to the next client and very rarely washed away the cum from their previous customer.

Not much repulses me, but a client who asked me to bring up phlegm and spit it into his mouth, where he swirled it around like a connoisseur of wine, did. Another offered me a lot of money not to wash myself for a whole week. He asked that it be left fishy, cheesy and rotten so he could 'make a meal out of it'. And you couldn't imagine this one:

a client wanted me to save all the condoms guys had blown into that day; he became highly aroused at seeing condoms full of cum. Because of the risk of disease, I dispose of all condoms immediately but he asked if he could take them home with him.

People reading this will wonder how I manage to assess a client's background and know they're not slinging me a line. If you're successful as a hooker you become very adept at drawing people out. You become a shrewd amateur psychologist and, where possible, I try to help men with their problems. I get men who cry, especially after separating from their wives. I told one client who burst into tears immediately after he entered my bedroom that perhaps he should see a counsellor. After his hour was over, he replied that I was far better than a doctor; he sees me often and we talk about his loneliness. Some guys are able to hold onto their emotions but cry when their defences are down immediately after an orgasm. When this happens I cuddle them and give them the feeling that they are loved. Not only do you have to be compassionate and understanding, but in some cases, a bloody good actress.

There was one client who was known around the brothels as 'the cowboy'. He was hairy all over and he dressed in a cowboy outfit, complete with spurs. The girls wouldn't go near him because it was said that he had crabs. 'Get the spotlight and check him for crabs,' they told me. Sure enough, his chest and pubic hair was riddled with crabs. He obviously had a psychiatric problem because during our conversations he would burst into tears. It is not unusual for men to become so twisted by their loneliness that they go to a brothel not only for sex but also for love and affection. As a result, they often become very emotional. I played the game with the cowboy and when he settled down he asked me what turned me on and what was my greatest fantasy as a prostitute. He wanted to satisfy me. I told him that I loved to sit in a corner while I watched a man tossing himself off. He thought that was great and happily pulled himself while I watched, and I was able to 'earn' my money without even touching him.

Hookers are in the game to make money and I've met a few who are more than happy to rip off clients. I know of one young man who spent $10 000 on a hooker who had him believing they were having a relationship—in a brothel, mind you! I remember saying to her, 'Do you have to kiss him?' and she said, 'Yes', screwing up her face, 'unfortunately.' She had no qualms about leading this guy on and taking his money. I believe he was a chef and frequently brought beautiful meals to her in the brothel. His father rang the brothel and pleaded with the receptionist not to let his son use his credit card anymore: the hooker had sent him broke.

Most girls who get into prostitution are reasonably straight, but it doesn't take long for some of them to become dishonest or liars. About eight years ago I had a client who paid $1000 for an all-night booking. Two of the girls in the studio disliked me intensely because I was so popular. When they thought the client and I were asleep they crept into the room and stole his wallet, which contained $300. Of course he later complained that his wallet was missing. The two girls blamed me, but they didn't know he'd been awake when they entered the room and saw them steal his wallet. Sometimes it's a dog-eat-dog world being a hooker, but occasionally justice prevails.

In another brothel the girls encouraged me to drink: they wanted me to make a fool of myself so they could take my clients and make more money. One of the girls spiked my wine with Rohypnol. I have only vague memories of what happened next, but I was told later that the girls laughed hysterically when I walked into the clients' waiting room with my dress inside out, lipstick all over my face, and a can's worth of hair spray on my hair. I woke up the next morning spread-eagled, with $500 strewn around my room. I thought, 'Christ, how on earth did I make this much money?' I could only remember hiccupping violently and trying to control myself while a client forcefully ground his body into my hip bones. It was agony lying there half-conscious wondering what the hell he was doing. He screwed me again and I continued to feel the pressure of his pelvic area digging into my body.

I soon learnt what this guy's caper was. My own interpretation of his actions was that he probably caught pubic lice from a prostitute and, in retaliation, decided to pass it on to another hooker. A week or so later I asked my ex-husband to check my cunt because it was so itchy. I spread my legs while he shone the torch on my pubic area and then, to my horror, he said, 'Babe, I think you've caught crabs.' I was devastated. I didn't want to look. I jumped into the bath, shaved the whole area, and doused myself with pubic lice lotion. I can't describe the revulsion I felt towards myself, knowing that a living creature was invading my body, crawling around, feeding off me, and making a nest in my pubic hair. Worse was to come: my ex-husband was not aware that he had to be treated as well and, even though we didn't engage in sexual intercourse for a few weeks, he caught crabs as well.

Prostitution is a risky business in brothels and escort agencies: not only is there the risk of disease; there is also the danger of physical assault. The risks are even greater for girls working from their own home or flat and there should be more protection. I'm not allowed to have another hooker working on my premises, yet if I were it could prevent me from being attacked. I know of one prostitute, who had been dropped off by her husband for an escort job, where the client believed she tried to steal money from his wallet and in anger threw her on the bed and literally bit off her nose. Her husband intervened and hit the client: he was given a 12-month good-behaviour bond for protecting his wife. The prostitute lost her assault case and, I believe, did not receive any compensation, although she subsequently needed extensive plastic surgery on her nose.

During an argument between two other girls, for no apparent reason a hooker's husband assaulted me outside a brothel some years ago. He grabbed me tightly around the neck, which was healing from recent cosmetic surgery, and caused such damage that I had to have further surgery. Another client, who became jealous of my sexual antics with other men, broke into my home at 2.30 in the morning and smashed everything in his path with a tyre lever. He assaulted me for three hours, stabbed clothing and bedding with a carving knife, tied a wet tea towel around my neck, and threatened to kill me. I was very lucky not to have been raped as well because I knew he was being treated for warts on his penis.

On a lighter note, recently a guy rang me and asked if we could have sex while another couple listened in on the telephone. I wasn't interested, but then he asked me if I was lactating by any chance, or did I know of any other girls in the industry who might be. It's not the first time I've been asked if I will breastfeed a client and treat him like a baby! I sometimes wonder if men ever grow up.

Prostitution through the centuries

A *Penthouse* article entitled 'Working Girls' gives a very succinct description of the profession of prostitution:

> There's no tougher, more maligned profession out there. Your office is a bed, your body the tools of trade. Your profession is the world's oldest, yet through a combination of misconception and puritanism, also one of its most reviled. To a total stranger you have to be a mother, a paramour or a friend giving of yourself in a way only lovers can do. Then you have to try to stay detached and maintain a regular life outside of work.

Peggy Miller, founder of the Canadian Organisation for the Rights of Prostitutes, was very frank in assessing her profession: 'What's wrong with fucking for a living?' She wasn't voicing her opinion for an off-beat magazine interview; she was speaking at a conference on the politics of prostitution and pornography, held in Toronto in November 1985. She went on to say, 'I like it, I can live out my fantasies, and I represent many other whores out there who, despite the terrible legal and social environment, enjoy their work.'

Not only the lonely and the perverted seek the solace of a prostitute: many famous personalities, even those with beautiful and desirable wives or partners, have been caught paying for sex, in spite of a public image of domestic contentment. A quick glance at history demonstrates that our forebears were equally adept at using their imagination to titillate the senses. Early literature, as far back as the fifth century BC, suggests that temple prostitution probably co-existed with commercial prostitution. Herodotus refers to temple prostitution in Babylon, where it seems every woman was required to sell her body in the name of religion:

> 'There is one custom amongst these people which is wholly shameful: every woman who is a native of the country must once in her life go and sit in the temple of Aphrodite and there give herself to a strange man. Once a woman has taken her seat she is not allowed to go home until a man has thrown a silver coin into her lap and taken her outside to lie with him.'

There must have been a line-up of young men and not-so-young men waiting to participate in this unusual rite.

In ancient Greece and Rome commercial prostitution was well established; and among the ruins of Pompeii there are paintings depicting services similar to those offered today. And, as today, some women became prostitutes because they enjoyed it. Messalina, wife of the Emperor Claudius, occasionally worked in Rome's brothels. She once threw out a challenge to regular workers to see who could screw the greatest number of men in a session. She won.

Kublai Khan, first emperor of the Mongol dynasty in China, provided prostitutes free of charge for foreign guests who visited his court. Marco Polo was one of the recipients of his famous hospitality and reported that the women were extremely beautiful. Most people with a religious bent look with reverence at the birth of Christ: in that year 36 000 prostitutes were registered in Rome. In early China, Greece, and Rome it was regarded as perfectly normal for young men to visit prostitutes.

King Solomon might have had the gift of patience and judgement, but he had hundreds of concubines to make sure he did not get too excited about the demands of decision making. His famous temple was filled with phallic symbols; in fact, it was little more than a brothel housing sodomites and whores.

In 1189 the French Crusaders took to the road with crosses on their shields and 350 'ladies' in case the Holy Land was indeed holy. And the Catholic Church isn't without guilt. In 1501 Pope Alessandro VI invited 50 prostitutes to a less-than-pious function: he had them strip and dance as God had brought them into the world and then watched his staff compete to screw the greatest number. Maybe he would have agreed with the current Pope's insistence on no contraception: it could ruin a man's pleasure!

In the 1830s there were more than 42 000 prostitutes registered in Paris and a particular feature of French brothels of the time was their sex shows. Apart from simulated lesbian scenes, many brothels also featured shows in which the women had sex with dogs. Up-market establishments used Great Danes; the 'suburban' brothels used Newfoundlands. One expensive Parisian brothel had a special apartment draped in black satin with silver ornamentation; in it a prostitute would lie on the bed with her face and body whitened to simulate the role of a corpse for necrophiles. Just 150 years ago in England there were nearly 800 whorehouses, apart from the thousands of woman scraping to make a living working the streets. New York at the same time was home to one prostitute for every seven men.

I believe most pragmatic people accept the reality of prostitution. Historically, the profession creates most controversy in societies that have taken a rigid stand on sex, either through legislation or through moral codes that favour marriage, monogamous relationships and the family. In the late 1960s and early 1970s the Queensland National Party Government, under the leadership of Jo Bjelke-Peterson, tried to enforce a repressive sexual code. Pictures in Brisbane's *Courier Mail* of policemen removing condom machines from the University of Queensland and government officials' insistence that prostitution did not exist in the city were laughable. It was zealotry at its worst, emanating from an out-of-touch premier.

When I worked as a journalist with Queensland Newspapers in the early 1970s, I, and nearly all the other journalists, knew that a few kilometres away in the Valley prostitution was rife. Brothels operated in the main street, with blatant advertising: it was obvious they were not selling lollypops. One wonders how many of those self-righteous pollies, or members of their 'loyal' police force, were recipients of sexual favours in exchange for turning a blind eye. It took until June 1999 for a more liberal Labor government to pass laws allowing 'boutique' brothels to operate. Even so, Jo's old party, maintaining its prudery, joined church groups in condemning the legalisation of brothels. And the Australian Family Association took out a newspaper advertisement urging cabinet to rethink! Why so many do-gooders continually try to remove, or at least deny the existence of, prostitution is beyond me.

Throughout history sex and power have proved a seductive combination. Women seek out powerful men for their own purposes; powerful men completely lose their heads over sensual young beauties. The classic case is that of Britain's Minister for War, John Profumo, who lied about sleeping with the 'delectable' Christine Keeler in the early 1960s. It happened that Keeler was on intimate terms with KGB operative and Russian naval attache Captain Eugene Ivanov. This 'just wasn't cricket', and the end result was the downfall of the Tory government. Although many critics took the moral high ground, one wonders whether there was a touch of jealousy because Keeler, then aged 19, was described as having 'exciting breasts and a figure which made men catch their breath with delight'. She denied in court being a prostitute but she undoubtedly accepted gifts in kind from a number of her paramours.

Again, it was sex and power in the ultra-conservative defence environment that kept the British tabloids ablaze in 1994, when Britain's former Chief of Defence Staff, Air Chief Marshal Sir Peter Harding, was caught in a liaison with Bienvenida Perez-Blanco, the

32-year-old wife of an ageing Tory MP. Bienvenida, described by the *Daily Express* as an ex-secretary with long legs and exotic looks, had 60-year-old Sir Peter spellbound. Worse, he broke a moral code condemning adultery, which he had issued to the defence force during his term in office. Tall, articulate and very charming, the defence chief even installed in his office a special 'love-line' for Bienvenida and, according to the *Express*, 'aired his views on government colleagues and secret defence deals to his lover'. On the day Sir Peter was appointed Chief of Defence Staff, the *Express* reported, he decided to celebrate with his inamorata. After a lunch of scallops and champagne at the Meridien Hotel, the increasingly amorous 60-year-old led Bienvenida to the lift. She told the *Express*, 'It started to go up and he took me in his arms, kissed me passionately and pressed against me and it was clear he was "very" aroused.' Unfortunately for Sir Peter, an outstanding pilot who had served on exchange with the RAAF and flown more than a hundred different aircraft types (including the Russian Su-27), a series of steamy love letters ensued: 'Every part of me cries out for you', 'You are my sun, my heaven, my light and my life', and the like. Eventually, Bienvenida's beleaguered husband found the letters and the coup de grace was delivered when the lovers met at the Dorchester Hotel, only to have their conversation recorded by a reporter and their last kiss captured by a photographer.

I recall a story told me by a retired RAAF fighter pilot, of an incident during a holiday in Japan, when he was a junior officer. Although no money changed hands, he still wonders what he was charged for a night's entertainment. In a club the pilot met a young Japanese woman who made it quite obvious that she was interested in him. Although he had no spare cash to provide a taxi to the next rendezvous she pushed aside his protestations, paid for the cab and the entrance to the next 'club'. He recalled he was taken to a luxurious room ablaze with light and decorated with wall-to-wall mirrors. Within a short time the naked nymphet was 'gasping and moaning' in a manner that convinced him he was on a par with the world's greatest lovers. He left the club suitably chuffed with his efforts, but it was only in the cold light of day that he wondered whether he was the entertainment behind one-way mirrors. Or whether he would one day suffer the embarrassment of seeing himself starring in a porn movie!

One has to question where the offering of 'generous gifts' ends and prostitution begins. The early North American Indians and indigenous occupants of New Guinea had no need of prostitutes. Both groups engaged in sexual activity from an early age. Gifts were proffered, but anthropologists see this as little different from the current practice of giving chocolates or flowers. But there was no need to buy sex.

Interaction with Europeans seems to make the difference. It is interesting to consider the experience of the Tahitians in 1769, when the British crew landed. Captain Cook recorded seeing the natives having sex in the open and noted that from the age of puberty Tahitian girls would have sex promiscuously, without guilt or embarrassment. Following pregnancy, the girls would usually marry and their activities were naturally curtailed, although evidence suggests that a husband would not necessarily be jealous if his wife had sex with another man. This guilt-free, open attitude to sex provided an environment free from perversion, but only until the Tahitians found you can put a price tag on sex.

The Tahitian girls treated the early visitors no differently and were puzzled and amused by the sight of sailors 'hot-footing' it into the forest to copulate because women were perfectly willing to make love publicly. Initially, small gifts were bestowed on the girls but it wasn't long before a less than subtle change took place and valuable 'goodies' for sex became the norm. Iron nails from the ship were especially prized. The ship's carpenter thus became a valued friend of the randy crew, but he soon ran out of the currency, causing many of the crew to surreptitiously remove nails from the wooden vessel. One suspects the pleasure of the moment was of far greater importance to the crew than the vessel's safety.

When visiting Tahiti in 1767, Captain Samuel Wallis noted in his journal,

> Chastity does not seem to be considered as a virtue among them, for they not only readily and openly trafficked with our people for personal favours, but were brought down by their fathers and brothers for that purpose; they were, however, conscious of the value of beauty, and the size of the nail that was demanded for the enjoyment of the lady was always in proportion to her charms.

Wallis admitted later that he was concerned that his ship, the *Dolphin*, would be pulled to pieces for the nails and iron holding it together. He was well aware that the early carefree sex in exchange for some small gift had turned into a more controlled enterprise: prostitution was in full swing. So, even in those adventurous, hedonistic days of early exploration of the Pacific a price came to be exacted for taking casual pleasure in a woman's body. But this exchange of 'goodies' for sex is not exclusive to humans: chimpanzees have been noted, in the wild and in the laboratory, exchanging food or tokens for sexual favours. And there is ample evidence that the use of money or goods in exchange for flesh has been around for thousands of years.

It is easy to understand that men who are not in a relationship or who suffer some disability that makes them unattractive to women would seek the services of a prostitute. Yet, as Liz observed and more formal surveys suggest, most clients are either married or in a stable relationship. It is occasionally suggested that promiscuous sex replaces our long-suppressed hunting instinct. Does that mean then that, to allow for a more contented partner, women should not only allow but encourage their men to pursue extracurricular relationships to satisfy their needs? Although mistresses are accepted in some societies, most women would object strongly to this idea.

Was 'war horse' sexologist Havelock Ellis right when he made the following observation in his book, *The Psychology of Sex*, first published in 1910:

> Even men who are happily married, are apt to feel, after some years of married life, a mysterious craving for variety.

> They are not tired of their wives, they have not the least wish or intention to abandon them, they will not, if they can help it, give them the slightest pain. But from time to time they are led by an almost irresistible and involuntary impulse to seek a temporary intimacy with a woman to whom nothing would persuade them to join themselves permanently.

Ellis might have said this almost 90 years ago, but nothing has really changed, even for the stammering, blushing and hugely successful Hugh Grant, star of *Four Weddings and a Funeral* and *Notting Hill*. Who could imagine he would need the services of a street prostitute when he had at home the gorgeous Liz Hurley. Grant weakened on a hot, steamy night in late June 1995. He was cruising along Hollywood's notorious Sunset Strip and stopped his white BMW to 'chat' with 23-year-old Divine Brown. She was dressed in regulation fishnet stockings, red top and mini-skirt. A price was agreed and Grant drove to a residential area, the street lights shaded by palm trees to give some privacy. When Divine's mouth was giving Hugh his opening dollars' worth a powerful torch illuminated the BMW. The vice squad officers decided Grant had not lowered his trousers and underpants simply to air his genitals in the fetid heat.

He and Divine were arrested for indulging in a 'lewd act'. And, while poor Hugh had failed to get his $60 worth, his hooker was suddenly onto a very healthy bonus (rumoured to be A$1 million) via the tabloids' appetite for sex scandals. Grant suffered the humiliation of being handcuffed, fingerprinted, and made to pose for a mug-shot before being charged. Meanwhile, in London one of the world's most desirable women, long-time girlfriend of the quintessential Oxford graduate, was about to have her world fall around her as quickly as Hugh had dropped his daks. Realising his awful blunder, Hugh rang Liz to break the news before issuing this statement: 'Last night I did something completely insane. I have hurt people I love and embarrassed people I work with. For both things I am more sorry than I can ever possibly say.'

Suffice to say, the tabloid press loved it! Both Hugh and Liz had much to lose because both their careers 'spun off' their relationship. If Liz had publicly dumped her partner would it have affected her career? Was, for example, her healthy contract with Estee Lauder assisted by all the hype associated with her close relationship with Grant and his very successful films? She could have had more reasons than love to forgive her philandering friend.

In an article in the UK publication *More*, Dr Patrick McGhee, head of psychology at Derby University, commented that there could be several reasons for Hugh's moment of insanity:

> Although Hugh has a beautiful girlfriend, he's been with her for nine years and maybe going to a prostitute was a way of recapturing lost sexual magic. Being successful, rich and becoming famous very quickly can lead to a search for new excitement. He might also have found the risk factor and the seediness thrilling or possibly it was a fantasy scenario.

Grant, of course, is not the only star to hire a hooker. Charlie Sheen admitted in an interview with *Movieline* magazine that he lost his virginity at the age of 15 by hiring a hooker and charging the $250 to his father's credit card. The star of *Platoon* and *The Three Musketeers* has not denied himself sexually, whether paying or not, and testified in July 1995 in videotaped evidence against Hollywood madam Heidi Fleiss to spending more than $33 000 on hookers, including treating himself to one on Christmas Day. Sheen's confession puts poor old Hugh in the shade, but many still would fail to understand why, while Hugh has the attention of one of the world's most beautiful women, he should succumb, albeit momentarily, to the attractions of a street hooker. Maybe Grant was 'inspired' by this paragraph in Ellis's book:

> The prostitute appeals by her fresh and natural coarseness, her frank familiarity with the crudest forms of life; and so lifts her customer for a moment out of the withering atmosphere of artificial thought and unreal sentiment in which so many civilised persons are compelled to spend the greater part of their lives.

To rub salt into the wound, when Grant's case was being heard there was a woman outside holding a large billboard on which was written, 'I would have paid you Hugh.' Still, there was some compensation for Grant: *Washington Post* columnist Tony Kornheiser noted on 'behalf' of Ms Hurley, 'Given what we know about British sex scandals, she should be happy. At least Grant was wearing men's underwear and the hooker was a woman.'

Grant was young and exceptionally handsome, but what about older, less appealing men? Take the comment of a 62-year-old respectably married man in Murtagh and Harris's intelligent study of prostitution, *Cast the First Stone:*

> Why is it that a prostitute can make me feel like a man, while my own wife can't? Sometimes after I go with a woman, I look at myself and say, Martin, are you really the man your family thinks is so great? You're not great, you're disgusting. And yet these girls make me feel good while I am with them. I forget everything else. It's like a dream. I watch TV and I see myself being a wonderful lover to a beautiful young girl. So I go out and pick up a prostitute. A fine end to my beautiful dream! I have never met a prostitute yet who was the kind of girl men dream about. But they do give me the illusion of being young again, for a little while.

I am reminded that most of my friend Liz's clients are married or in a stable relationship. I've heard numerous calls on her answering system saying to ring only between certain times 'because my missus [or partner] might take the call'. Yet Liz believes these men are in most respects happily married and just want a change or an adrenalin charge. Does it follow that a visit to a hooker is one of the few avenues left for illicit excitement for a 'down-trodden and domesticated' but sexually adventurous male? Liz thinks this is the case. She says a high percentage of her clients fit Ellis's description. Apart from men with unusual fetishes, most are content with their lot. The last thing they want is an emotionally charged female they picked up in a bar or club ringing their home wanting to know if the soothing and loving words they used as levers to remove her knickers are true. Emotional involvement beyond marriage or partnership is just too complicated. As Liz says, most clients weigh up the odds. The money spent on drinks, dinner, and maybe flowers, with no guarantee of a screw at the end of the night, does not make sense. A prostitute delivers the goods without the complications.

But what about the prostitutes? Is money all they get out of the brief encounter? They are usually seen as the victims yet Zoe, a former prostitute and at the time of interview a member of the Australian Prostitute's Collective, told reporter Roberta Perkins,

> There is a certain amount of power in straight sex situations because the guys are nervous. They are paying for you, and you can demand what you want and don't want: no you can't kiss me, no you can't do that, time's up, whatever. In my personal experience I found it was a total role reversal to the usual men in positions of power and dominance and women subservient to them, and I gained a lot of confidence out of it.

A spokeswoman for American prostitutes, Margo St James, who founded COYOTE (Call Off Your Old Tired Ethics) in 1973, went even further:

> The great fear for men, who are running things, is that if whores have a voice, suddenly good women are going to find out how much their time is worth and how to ask for money. In fact, I've always thought that whores were the only emancipated women.

We have not reached a state of nirvana, where everyone has equal rights, sexually or otherwise. French prostitute Anna Salva gives us a telling insight into the bubbling cauldron of perversions that she believed would surface following the forced closure of Paris brothels in 1946:

> The majority of our customers, most of them middle class, were unbalanced, obsessed or vicious. According to my own experience and that of my colleagues, at least 40 per cent of brothel clients are sexually abnormal. When we

closed we asked one another, with malicious amusement, to which of these respectable ladies who had voted to close the brothels, the various sadists, flagellants, chain-maniacs and ludicrous masochists who had come to us would now turn? While we were packing, we kept thinking of the incest-oriented clients we had always to remember to call 'Dad' unless they happened to be characters who called us 'Mother' or by the name of one of their sisters—not to mention the frequent visitors who, not daring to approach boys, forced us women to play Adonis to them. All those prosperous citizens, respectfully saluted throughout the neighbourhood—tender husbands and affectionate fathers, arrogant lawyers, eminent doctors and eloquent politicians—were in truth mentally sick. For the most part their wives had no idea of the nature and degree of their aberrations. It was only of us that they dared make their appalling demands.

Many of the practices clients need to achieve orgasm can be only be described as bizarre. Havelock Ellis cites a case where the client could reach orgasm only by watching a naked girl wring the neck of a pigeon. And in San Francisco in the late eighteenth century Madame Gabrielle's exclusive houses could offer peep-hole sex, black men performing with white girls (shocking at the time), and even a double act with a Shetland pony.

In Australia's capital city I have yet to hear of a case involving a horse, but perversion is alive and well. The genteel city of Canberra is not only the centre for 'hot air' from our federal politicians; it is also the centre for 'hot sex' because it is home to the nation's largest distributors of pornographic videos. Prostitution is legal; most of the brothels are in the light-industrial areas of Fyshwick and Mitchell. So while you have your Honda serviced or your Ping golf clubs regripped you can treat your body.

A 1991 report by a Select Committee of the Australian Capital Territory Legislative Assembly found that seven brothels were operating in the Territory (there are now considerably more). Not included were the numerous escort agencies. The Select

Committee also found that prostitution in the Territory was relatively drug free and that the average cost for a half-hour session was $80. It said, '... most of the workers we met appear to be self-assured, articulate, outgoing, and enjoying their work.' (It would have been interesting to question the Committee about its criteria for this assessment.) The report also supported Liz's observations about the men who seek the services of hookers:

> What kind of men seek out prostitutes? The simple answer is every kind of man: the old and the young, working class and middle class, wealthy and not so wealthy. For some men, such as the lonely, the ugly or the incapacitated, prostitutes are the only person to have sex with. One thing that does seem clear is that very many men going to prostitutes are married.

Liz. (Photo by Exclusive Photography Canberra Pty Ltd.)

Ray's keys, which were accidentally locked in his light truck, suddenly appeared in Liz's bedroom after the pair had sex.

Spirit writings on Liz's fridge door.

The journalist who broke the Humpty Doo story – Litchfield Times editor, Jack Ellis.

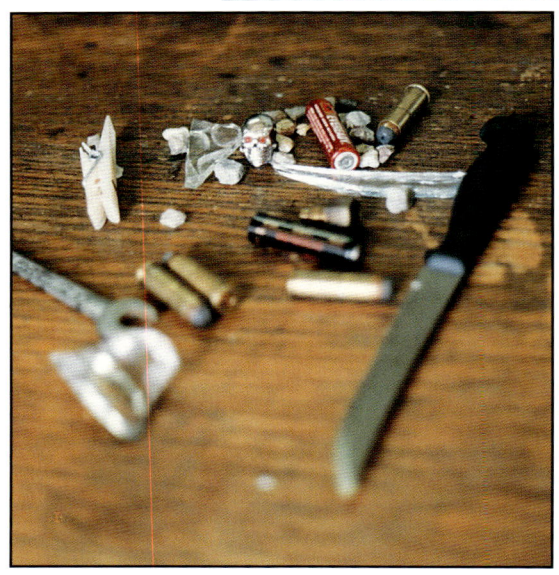

Some of the assorted objects including a steak knife, bullets and batteries that were transformed into 'flying missiles' by the poltergeist. (Photo by Tony Healy).

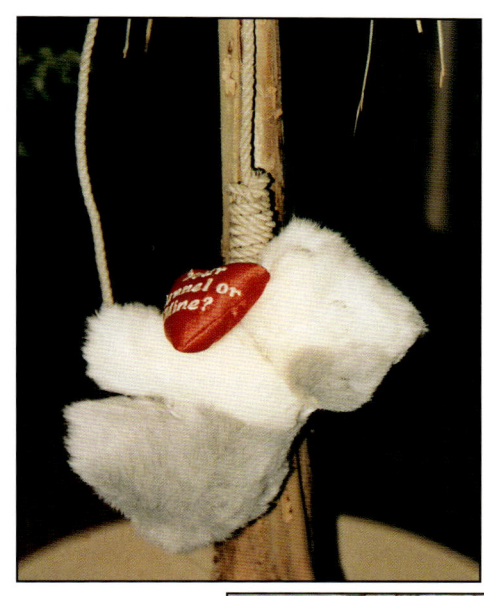

Attached to the 'hangman's noose' the toy dog with a heart attached to its mouth with the message 'your kennel or mine'. It 'appeared' during the height of psychic activity in Liz's house.

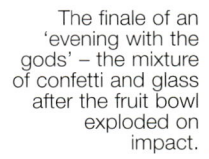

The finale of an 'evening with the gods' – the mixture of confetti and glass after the fruit bowl exploded on impact.

Some of the objects which appeared from 'nowhere' in Liz's house during the height of the spirit activity.

The Humpty Doo house in the Northern Territory that attracted the most amazing poltergeist activity. (Photo by Tony Healy).

Andrew Clarke's partner, Kirsty Agius was accused by Channel 7 journalist Greg Quail, of throwing a plastic lid for the cameras – a charge she vehemently denied.

'Murph' cn his long suffering Kwaka. He amazed the other residents by not thumping cynical journalists. (Photo by Tony Healy).

An evening with the gods

The date was Tuesday 20 December 1994—five days before Christmas. It was a hot, oppressive evening: Canberra had had its hottest day for 20 years and the air conditioning where I worked, in the nine-storey Defence building, was unable to cope. I'd been delighted to leave work just after 5 pm.

My old Subaru was like a sauna and I was looking forward to jumping on my Triumph and going for a ride to cool off, rather than visiting Liz for more phenomena. At home I had a quick bite to eat before donning my lightest summer-weight bike gear and hauling the bike out of the garage. It was still bloody hot and humid, with the possibility of a storm. As usual I enjoyed the 20-kilometre ride, especially the cooling 100 kph section, to Liz's house in Theodore, part of Canberra's so-called Nappy Valley.

When I parked the bike a neighbour looked suspiciously at me. He must have seen my Triumph there many times and wondered how I could afford such frequent contact! Residents near Liz were well aware of her activities, which did not endear her to them. (This could have been why they didn't rush to the rescue when they heard Liz and Donna scream later that night.) I removed the key and glanced at the bike, to make sure it was properly supported on its centre stand, before walking up the driveway. The heat had made me tired and, as I knocked on Liz's door, I was hoping I wouldn't doze off in her bedroom while waiting for the elusive spirits to act. I had my small pocket radio with me because broadcaster Chris Wisby was running a series of my 'ghost stories' on the ABC and I wanted to listen to his show. Basically, I was going through the motions, especially since Liz had insisted that something special would happen tonight. At least, excusing myself to listen to Chris's broadcast would give me an opportunity to wrap the evening up early.

The proceedings started with the three of us chatting around the kitchen table, drinking orange juice. Donna, as usual, was nervously chain smoking. Liz was excited, expecting something to happen, and took little notice when I mentioned the radio broadcast. I, on the other hand, was non-committal and felt totally relaxed—too relaxed really—when we walked into her bedroom at about 8.30 pm. This time we weren't going to wait for the small-time activity on the kitchen table. Before I sat down I walked around the bedroom to make sure there were no wires, strings or anything else that might create activity. I doubt the KGB, the CIA or ASIO would have awarded me a diploma for my de-bugging efforts, but anyway I could see nothing untoward. Surprisingly, Liz had cleaned her bedroom and neither the condoms nor the huge black vibrator, which were normally kept close by, were anywhere to be seen.

After my search I sat on a small cane chair opposite Liz and Donna, who were sitting on the bed as they had during my previous visit. The weather, combined with the permanently blocked window and heavy blind, made the atmosphere positively sauna-like when Liz closed the door. Again I thought, 'Don't doze off, you silly bastard, or you'll embarrass yourself in front of the girls.' I needn't have worried. To create the right conditions, Liz switched off the bedroom globes; there was only sufficient ambient light for me to see the girls' silhouettes. I sat quietly and waited. With my head bowed and my eyes closed, I tried to put myself in a meditative state, naively believing this would attract the spirits.

As my dream state shifted towards a doze I heard an explosive crack, similar to a rifle shot, followed by a loud thump against the bedroom wall. It scared the daylights out of me. The girls screamed as though confronted by their last moments. My immediate reaction was to assume we were being shot at by a jealous boyfriend or a furious client. I didn't have a clue where the noise came from but quickly realised it was unlikely to be a bullet: there was no shattering of glass and if anyone was trying to scare or shoot us they were unlikely to aim into the brick wall. It seemed as though the explosion was in the bedroom, which of course was ridiculous.

Regardless, my pulse was racing and I was well and truly awake. When she recovered, Liz rushed over and turned on the overhead light, which was fitted with a normal white globe. Immediately I took a quick look around the room but all I could see was a potato on the floor. I picked it up and inspect it—it was an ordinary potato sprouting shoots. My mind was in overdrive and I soon recalled Liz's hairdresser and her social worker both mentioning the appearance of a sprouting potato. How could the potato have got there? One of the girls could have thrown it on the floor but if they did how did they simultaneously make the noise like a rifle crack. I tried to think through the options logically but I was getting considerably more questions than answers. Liz and Donna meanwhile were gabbling like a pair of excited, frightened schoolgirls: they certainly weren't showing signs of having set up that little act to con me.

And that little act was only the beginning of the most extraordinary evening I have experienced during my research into the paranormal.

I racked my brains, trying to work out the source of the noise, and in a moment of frustration picked up the potato and threw it against the bedroom wall, somehow expecting the same 'explosion'. All I got was a dull thud, as you would expect. I saw the potato roll away from the plasterboard wall and under the bed. Liz was impatient to continue, so she reached over to switch off the light. Before her fingers touched the switch a gold-coloured rock appeared from 'nowhere' and rolled along the floor. Liz shrieked with excitement. I picked up the rock and was surprised to find that it was warm to the touch. I recalled the hairdresser mentioning the appearance of 'gold-coloured river stones'. Liz didn't seem to think the rock was of any great significance and was again keen to move on to more interesting 'activities'.

I sat on the cane chair and put the rock by my feet. Liz switched off the light. Within seconds there was a blinding flash above and behind the girls' heads and a another 'rifle crack'. Again I wondered if I was wrong and somebody was firing a gun at close range. The girls screamed even more loudly and I felt my heart pounding: this was getting frightening. Immediately I switched on the light and there on the bed was a smoking fire cracker with an activated release string. I knew the girls could have activated the cracker but they were genuinely frightened as opposed to being excited by a set-up prank. Besides, the 'sound' was not consistent with the bang produced by that type of cracker. I picked it up and examined it. On the outside of the plastic case was written 'Champagne Party Popper'. I found out later this Chinese-made cracker is readily available; identical versions were used for my niece Meaghan's twenty-first birthday party in Brisbane some six months later. But in retrospect there is one interesting difference. All the 'poppers' in Brisbane were filled with small streamers. When I returned to Canberra I examined the cracker again: on the side it read, 'Flame-proof with streamers—contains 0.25 grams of powder or less.' The popper that night had no streamers.

Liz and Donna were really hyped up. I was trying to stay cool and detached because I knew it was very important to observe everything as closely as possible. While the light was on, and to give me 'breathing space', I asked Liz for a torch so that I could retrieve the potato from under the bed. As she bent down to help me search under the low-set bed she replied that there wasn't a torch in the house. At that instant a small red object, which at first appeared to be a cigarette lighter, fell on the floor beside us. Donna, grasping to make sense of the situation, immediately claimed it was her cigarette lighter, a not unreasonable suggestion because on a previous visit Donna's lighter, which had been in the kitchen, suddenly 'appeared' in the bedroom. But this wasn't Donna's lighter: it proved to be an Eveready torch about the same size as a lighter. It looked brand new and worked perfectly, and I used it to recover the potato. Now I was faced with the realisation that this unseen force, regardless of whether Liz believed it was one of her spirit friends or not, had an intelligence.

I thought that was the end of the activity for the night and sat on Liz's bed trying to make sense of it all. On my last visit the cigarette lighter had lit in mid-air; tonight the cracker had been activated in mid-air, apparently by an invisible force. I shook my head—it was impossible! Liz was still completely manic and wanted to continue. Donna was unsure and frightened. For me that was enough for the time being. I had the excuse of wanting to listen to the radio broadcast and asked Liz and Donna if they minded if we went back to the kitchen for a breather, to have a drink and to listen to my interview. There was more than a little irony in listening to my 'ghost stories' on the radio while here the real thing was happening.

As I gulped down a soft drink and waited for Chris's program to come on I noticed on Liz's fridge a drawing in pink lipstick of a skull and crossbones and two opposing parallel lines with a cross in the left-hand corner. Liz had told me many times about the noughts and crosses, so I guess this was a gentler part of the night's entertainment. More importantly, those drawings were not on the fridge earlier in the evening. I ambled into the loungeroom, curious to see if 'games' were still being played, and was taken aback by the next revelation. Confetti was lying on the floor, making a ring around a dog lead. Within moments Liz shouted out that there was a toy puppy strung up in one of her pot plants with a noose around its neck. And as I wandered across to inspect this latest finding a plastic bone appeared from nowhere. Then out of the corner of my eye I saw a door knob roll along the floor, quickly followed by confectionery in the shape of two edible frogs, one green and the other red. I went back into the bedroom to see if anything else had happened—sure enough, another sprouting potato manifested itself and rolled along the bedroom floor, silently this time.

Something or someone was playing extraordinary games. We all recalled that Liz's bull terrier, Piggy, had barked while we were in the bedroom. Normally an exuberant, excitable dog with enormous strength, Piggy was now uncharacteristically quiet, walking around the loungeroom very timidly, as though suffering some sort of shock, and steering well clear of the confetti and the dog lead. She treated other objects with similar caution, as though fearful that they might hurt her. Liz offered her the toy puppy that she'd found in the pot plant. Piggy sniffed it warily for some time before grabbing it by the scruff of the neck and trotting away. This was totally out of character for the dog, who, according to Liz, takes immediate, fearless pleasure in playing with any object offered.

For me, it was time out from the inexplicable happenings. I turned on my radio to listen to Chris Wisby's broadcast. I always enjoy Chris's programs because of his easy-going, engaging manner. He worked for me as an officer in the RAAF Specialist Reserve and his easy-going nature extended to his dress. He was chastised about this by a female officer during his initial training course, but because she admitted to being 'besotted' by his voice the brief was less than effective. That's Chris.

While I was listening to the radio I heard rain on the roof and asked Liz if I could park my Triumph in the carport. She readily agreed because she knew how fussy I was with the bike. Opening the front door, I stumbled on a pile of rocks on the doormat. I called out to Liz and Donna but neither of them had an explanation. They were definitely not there when I arrived. I stepped over the rocks and walked down the slope, my mind stunned by what was going on. When I was about halfway down the driveway a small rock hit me in the middle of my back. Not hard. Just hard enough to make sure I would take note. I turned around and asked the girls if they'd thrown the rock. They started laughing when I told them what had happened: they hadn't seen anything because it was dark and raining. Sure, they could have thrown the rock, but what a shot—square between the shoulder blades. 'Its' precision continued.

When I reached the bike there was more to mystify me. There, in the middle of my seat and exactly in the middle of the petrol filler cap, were two gold-coloured rocks, the same colour as the pair that 'appeared' in the bedroom. I called out to the girls to check out the latest 'findings'. Liz raced down the driveway and yelped, 'I told you so!' Not for the first time did I wonder what the neighbours thought about all this raucous behaviour. Liz was ecstatic and didn't care what commotion she caused. Her spirit friends were her life and they were not letting her down.

The rain was getting heavier so I pocketed the gold rocks, turned the ignition key, and gently thumbed the starter button. I am particularly fond of my bike and give it VIP treatment. It is always clean and polished and serviced right on time. There is considerable commonsense to this approach: you need everything in your favour when you are riding a high-powered bike. Except for difficult cold-weather starting (resolved later by replacing the bike's black box), the Triumph is very reliable, yet when the engine kicked over it immediately revved uncontrollably. Although startled, I quickly switched off the ignition. This had never happened before. I checked the choke and snapped open the hand throttle a few times in an attempt to clear any obstruction that might be jamming the carbs. Same result. Liz started laughing, but I was pissed off: I don't like my bike being fiddled with, by earthbound hands or by malevolent forces. I suspected Liz had set me up with the help of a knowledgeable friend and I told her of my suspicions in no uncertain terms.

Liz knew I was angry but, still laughing, conceded she had pleaded with her spirit friends to 'do something to my bike.' Her suggestions had been 'either let a tyre down or empty the petrol tank'. Well, I wasn't a happy investigator. Yes, it was okay to be a neutral observer but stuffing around with my bike was not

'Queensberry Rules'. I left the bike and went back to the house, feeling very irritated and in no mood for any further surprises. Back at the house things were still happening. The kitchen's cold water tap had been turned on full blast and before our eyes a branch was ripped off one of the hanging plants and the basket left swinging. How was it done? I didn't know and at that moment I didn't care because I was developing a humdinger of a headache.

I hung around the kitchen for another five minutes or so while more strange things happened. What would have set my interest alight two hours ago now had no meaning. My mind was elsewhere—I wanted to know what was wrong with my bike. Practical concerns, such as how was I to get home and should I leave the bike at Liz's, came to mind. 'It' was getting to me. I jogged down the driveway in the rain and tried a few more times, but still the rev counter swung around wildly towards the red line. This was crazy. In desperation I went around to the left-hand side of the bike and turned the throttle-stop screw back half a dozen turns and tried again. Sure enough, the comforting, slightly off-beat rumble of the big triple returned to a sensible 1000 rpm idle. I was much relieved but still brooding on whether Liz had set up the 'throttle jamming'. I walked back up the driveway, my head throbbing by now with pain.

Supported by Donna, I told Liz it was time to quit—enough was enough. Liz protested. She was just getting into her stride and insisted there was going to be one last spectacular event. Frankly, I had lost interest but I followed her dutifully into the bedroom, where she mentally asked her spirit friend if he had fiddled with my bike. The spirit replied in the affirmative. The three of us returned to the kitchen and I cursed myself for not bringing a camera—I needed photographic evidence. I knew Liz couldn't keep the confetti on the floor so we swept it up and poured the contents of the dustpan into a large glass fruit bowl that we placed on the kitchen table. I also gathered up the other evidence—potatoes, pocket torch, gold rocks, the cracker, the dog lead, the lollies and the toy puppy.

Liz pleaded with me to stay, but my head hurt and I'd had enough.

She was still trying to convince me there would be one more spectacular event as I pulled on my motor cycle jacket. My arm was barely through the jacket sleeve when there was another deafening crack, similar to the one we experienced in the bedroom. The confetti-filled bowl flew one-and-half metres off the kitchen table and smashed into hundreds of pieces in front of the fridge. My headache forgotten for a moment, I was intrigued—not only by the shattering of the bowl but also by the fact that there were so few large fragments of glass. Some were a couple of centimetres long but most were so small it was as though the bowl had been hurled with enormous force into a solid object. Or had the glass had been transformed through some process to allow the multiple fractures to occur? I was completely flummoxed. We gathered up the pieces, and poor Donna picked up a sharp splinter in her foot. Removal of the offender gave me my exit cue. I didn't want to hang around any longer. I could only liken the 'force' to the behaviour of an excited child—the more it was encouraged the worse it got.

I knew as I walked down the driveway with Liz and Donna that I would eventually look back in wonder at the evening's events but right then I wanted to get home and relax with a beer. As if to give me a final farewell, whoever or whatever it was had not finished: both mirrors on my bike had been cranked 30 degrees inwards. Without giving it a great deal of thought, I pushed the mirrors out to their correct position and gently thumbed the starter, half expecting the uncontrollable revving again. But no—the engine behaved normally. I waved goodbye and rode home cautiously, wondering if anything else was going to happen, especially a jammed throttle.

By the time I arrived home the headache was worse and in my confusion I tried to flick the centre stand down instead of the side stand before opening the garage door. When I realised what I had done I removed my foot to flick down the side stand but it was already down. The side stand always makes a slight bang as the spring-operated lever hits the stop: this time there was no sound. The engine had been turned off and I could have easily heard the 'thump' through the helmet. I shrugged, pushed the Triumph into the garage and heaved it onto its centre stand. I spent a few minutes examining the bike before I was satisfied the forces had not made any other adjustments that could endanger me.

I wandered to the front door, knowing I had to write down the basic details of the evening. Before turning on my Mac I opened the fridge, grabbed a bottle of Cascade, and slumped into my reclining chair. After downing the beer I decided I needed to 'offload', so I spoke to my sister in Brisbane. Always understanding about my paranormal adventures, she agreed it had been an extraordinary series of events. Finally, I left the comfort of the chair and went to my desk to record 'an evening with the gods'.

* * *

During the next few months I spent many weeks researching poltergeist activity in Australia and overseas; I also talked to leading parapsychologists in the United Kingdom. I found out, for example, that stone throwing is not unusual: there are numerous instances of poltergeists doing it. An unusual case was reported in the *London Times* in January 1843. Two young French girls were picking up leaves in the commune of Livet, France, when, without any apparent cause, stones of different colours began falling on them. The frightened girls rushed off to get their parents, who were also greeted with a shower of stones. Many people, among them members of the clergy and doctors, witnessed the phenomenon, which continued for several days but only when the girls were in a particular spot. In 1998 I investigated a case where rock throwing was a commonplace activity in an extraordinary case at Humpty Doo, near Darwin.

But the aspects of the evening with Liz and Donna that really intrigued me were the 'rifle cracks' associated with the appearance of the potato, the firecracker and the destruction of the glass bowl. Liz later told me that unusual incidents in the brothels were often accompanied by the same 'rifle crack' noises. Thumbing through a number of works in a Canberra library, I came across an intriguing reference. Famous Swiss psychologist Carl Gustav Jung wrote, in his book, *Memories, Dreams, Reflections*, 'Something happened which was destined to influence me profoundly: a report like a pistol shot which turned out to have been caused by table-top splitting in two.' Jung recalled that he was thunderstruck. He couldn't come up with a reasonable explanation of how a 70-year-old table of solid walnut could split on a summer day in conditions of high humidity. Jung said his mother, who was knitting at the time, was flabbergasted and dropped her knitting in fright, believing the 'explosion' was an omen of future events.

Two weeks later, Jung's mother, his sister and the maid witnessed another 'deafening report' that left them all in a state of great agitation. The noise had come from the direction of the sideboard and Jung spent some time trying to ascertain the cause. He eventually found a bread knife that had been in the sideboard had snapped into several pieces. On questioning the family, he was told the knife had been used late that afternoon and had been returned to the sideboard. Apparently no one had been to the sideboard in the intervening hours. Jung took the remains of the knife to the best cutlers in town and they examined it under a magnifying glass. Jung was assured that it could not have snapped accidentally: it must have been broken by human intervention. Jung was shaken: 'I was completely at a loss and could offer no explanation of what had happened, and this was all the more annoying as I had to admit I was profoundly impressed,' he said.

Why and how had the knife broken and the table split? The hypothesis that it was just a coincidence went much too far. Recognition that some unexplained force had caused the 'pistol cracks' and the resultant physical phenomena led Jung to consult a medium and to develop a lifetime interest in the paranormal.

But what about the manifestations? Examples abound in the literature on psychic phenomena, but let us look at Indian guru Sai Baba, who has been studied by numerous scientists and parapsychologists. Sai Baba came to the attention of parapsychologists Erlunder Haraldsson and Karlis Osis, both of whom were highly sceptical about teleportation and apports until they met the spiritual leader in the 1970s in Andhra Pradesh. Baba refused to undergo formal tests because he told the pair he used his powers only to help disciples in trouble. But he did grant them a number of interviews, during which he 'unveiled' *viputi* (holy ash) and a gold ring. Both researchers said the 'appearances' were along the lines of palming techniques used by conjurers. Baba then caused a picture in a ring he had given Osis to vanish, although the ring was so constructed that the picture could not have fallen out. He also materialised a bulky necklace that both researchers concluded could not have been palmed.

Haraldsson and Osis witnessed 20 'appearances' or 'situations' of a paranormal nature and were further impressed by the sheer volume of Sai Baba's 'activity' in the past 40 years. The holy ash, which he distributed on his walks, would be easily detectable, as would the oil and other liquids, if he had to pull it out from any place in his clothing. The researchers were careful to eliminate this possibility. Haraldsson and Ossis admitted in the January 1977 *Journal of the American Society for Psychical Research*, 'We realise that without adequate experimental conditions the evidence will never be conclusive.' They hoped, however, that 'the variety and richness of the phenomena associated with Sai Baba may provide unique research opportunities for both Western and Indian scientists.'

As happened to Jung, my experience affected me profoundly and, like Jung, I was equally anxious to find answers. Elsewhere I discuss other incidents, in Australia and elsewhere, that reinforce the evidence I have gathered. The amazing case at Humpty Doo is of particular interest because the phenomena were witnessed by more than 40 people, from priests to police.

Extraordinary witness reports

I still needed further proof, so I asked Liz if she could give me some contacts—other people who had experienced unusual happenings in her presence or through her influence. Like other investigators of the paranormal, I constantly questioned my own awareness, my own judgment. It was only through overwhelming evidence from other sources that I became confident that I was not being hypnotised or the victim of a magician gifted with amazing skills. In all, I interviewed nine people: Liz's partner; her closest friend; a former prostitute who had worked with Liz; Liz's hairdresser; a social worker; a Canberra policeman; a construction worker; Liz's mother; and, because of the paranormal nature of the investigation, one person who was a discarnate entity speaking through medium Monica Hamers. What follows describes their experiences.

Johnny is Liz's partner. He has the brooding good looks men envy and women find irresistible, yet he is also a sensitive, likeable young man in his twenties who says he had considered a lifetime of celibacy and service as a Dominican priest. Not surprising, when one becomes of his strong, self-imposed Catholic faith.

Discipline was instilled through prayer sessions that could last up to three hours a day. I'm sure his friends don't see him as the type of man who would need, or indeed seek, the services of a prostitute. Johnny bravely confides, though, that his obsession with Catholicism also caused him to have extreme guilt feelings about sex. He did not want to cause himself or a girlfriend stress, and so sought the ministrations of a prostitute in an attempt to sort himself out. After one session with Liz he says he came under her spell—a spell that allowed him to express his sexuality and to put into balance his terrible guilt about anything to do with the senses. Over the months he developed strong feelings for Liz, beyond the client–prostitute boundary. The pair developed a highly unusual relationship: Liz enjoyed the attention and caring provided by her young lover while Johnny found life with Liz an amazing experience. Prostitution can be a very lonely business and, as Liz often stressed, everyone needs a loving relationship.

Johnny is an intelligent, incisive thinker and his relationship with Liz had not coloured his memory when he recounted what he experienced in Liz's bedroom, again with Donna there too. His scepticism is very real, yet as we talked it became apparent that his experiences were very similar to mine. For example, in her bedroom at around 3 pm on a Tuesday in mid-November 1994 Liz asked her spirit friends Marty and Ben to demonstrate their powers. Johnny said that before the session started he'd been apprehensive, even scared, about what might happen through tapping in to the spirits' powers. But his curiosity won and he was fascinated about the possible outcome. He wasn't disappointed. In the space of half an hour Donna was 'slapped' on the face by an unseen 'hand', which left a red mark; vitamin pills were thrown on the floor; an aerosol container was thrown on the floor beside him; a lamp was knocked over by unknown forces; and a butter knife landed in his lap. Again, potatoes appeared, and two or three small ones were thrown against the wall with considerable force.

After witnessing this demonstration of psychic energy, Johnny was still not convinced. 'I thought it must have been some trick', he said.

In spite of seeing the whole thing with my own eyes, I thought I was being conned or, worse, that I was simply gullible. I had closed my mind to what I'd seen. When I expressed my scepticism to Liz she was furious and asked me to leave the house immediately because she is so sensitive about her spirit friends. Of course, I later recognised my reaction was inappropriate and we were soon back together. But there is one aspect that has me completely stumped. The aerosol container, the butter knife and the vitamin pills were not in the bedroom before we started the experiment—they were in the kitchen. I checked Liz's bedroom before the session and I'm convinced those three objects weren't there. How they got there I don't know because the bedroom door was closed and the light was on.

Liz's hairdresser is another witness who gives the phenomena credibility. Nicole, 43 and mother of three teenage children, owns and runs a hairdressing salon in one of Canberra's suburban shopping centres. She is happily married, although her husband is not into 'spooks and ghosts' and refuses to discuss things related to paranormal activity. Nicole said that in the hairdressing business you become a bit of an amateur psychologist and customers often tell you the most intimate and strange stories. But none touches what she and her staff experienced when Liz arrived for an appointment for blonde streaks in September 1994. Nicole had already seen Liz's 'wizardry', when a brush or some other small object would 'find another home' in the salon or the radio would turn on or off before Liz rang for an appointment.

On the September day in question business was light, which meant the staff were able to give the four clients who were there a little extra attention. One young mother wanted her two-year-old's hair cut. While Liz waited and chatted with Nicole the mother lifted the child out of its stroller and onto a chair. 'Within minutes the stroller was turned on its side,' Nicole exclaimed..

I suppose we were surprised because no person or force was present to turn the stroller over. One of my staff righted the pram. Shortly after, it was upturned again—except this time backwards. Again, nobody took a great deal of notice, although the mother was obviously worried. The salon has an open entrance so when a potato rolled in we thought it was kids playing games. I went outside and looked on both sides of the walkway, but there was no one there.

We started getting nervous when a flat river stone, painted gold, was suddenly thrown into the salon. I guess we were a little frightened, but we rationalised that it was kids mucking about. Again we looked outside but there was no one there: it appeared to have come from nowhere. Next, another potato suddenly materialised, with broken sticks piercing its skin. Liz reckoned later that they were incense sticks from her house. But what really upset my staff, and the clients, was another gold-covered rock was thrown in and, for a few seconds, jumped around the floor with an energy of its own. My staff started to really get spooked and I knew my clients would start screaming if I did nothing. I knew Liz was the cause. It was even worse when small pieces of rolled bark started falling 'through' the ceiling and a five cent coin appeared at a client's foot. Finally, one nervous client got up the courage to ask what was going on. I gave her some weak excuse about kids fooling around, but I know she wasn't convinced. One of my girls said she felt somebody breathing on her neck, which really scared her, and then a little gold-coloured key fell at her feet.

I was getting very concerned by this stage. Not only were we all scared, but If word got around about these experiences the publicity would be very bad for my business. I did the only thing I thought would solve the problem: I went up to Liz and told her to get out—now! Liz, as usual, was excited by what was going on and wanted hair rollers to be thrown around as well. My voice became more heated and I told her to go: that's enough. She wanted me to listen to the spirit voices on her tape, but she finally relented and left. She went straight to the local food barn to shop but, as she walked through the lines of produce, cans of food 'mysteriously' fell off behind her.

If I remember correctly the whole episode took about 25 minutes. My staff were confused and frightened, and they insisted that all the evidence should be collected and thrown away. On reflection, I have no idea how these objects appeared, but I know they did. We all observed the event and I'm convinced that Liz was the catalyst.

Nicole does not criticise Liz for engaging in prostitution. 'Some say she is a bit of a bully but this aspect of her personality probably comes from under-confidence,' she said. 'I think she needs these spirit friends as a bolster to her self-esteem.'

Peta has known Liz for a number of years. They first met when they worked as prostitutes at Canberra's Golden Apple brothel. An attractive, aware young woman in her mid-twenties, Peta got out of the game after earning enough money to set up her own business as a natural therapist. 'Liz could handle prostitution better than me', Peta admitted.

You learn to play a part and act, but most of all you had to fake really well. The difference between us is she really likes sex. Yes, I occasionally enjoyed it but very few clients were like Tom Cruise. Even though I could earn $3000 a week, in the end I was glad to give it away—it became too stressful and ageing.

Peta also experienced the antics of Liz's spirit friends. 'I thought Liz was a bit loopy when we met: she seemed so over the top,' she said.

But now I really believe she is very brave. Liz was frequently ignored by the other girls, not only because of the disturbances but also because she was bloody good at her job and the clients invariably came back. But management couldn't handle the potential adverse publicity and the loss of business associated with her spirit activities. It didn't worry Liz: she still kept up the contact with her spirit friends, regardless. When Liz was working, paper clips and pens dropped on the floor from nowhere. Vases and flower pots would fall over for no reason. I had paper clips thrown at my back and Liz used to say, 'Don't worry. They just want to tell you they're around.' Door knobs would turn without assistance. Doors would open and shut by themselves. I was scared—it was like being on a big dipper when you were screaming to get off, yet when you were on the ground you couldn't wait to go for another ride. It was both exciting and scary.

One night I could feel a ghost there. You couldn't see it, but you knew it was there. Another evening we were watching television, waiting for clients, and a pen dropped in my lap. No one there could have thrown it in my lap: it just appeared. And often Liz would ask Marty to ring the phone and 'it' did. I answered it once and it was just dead, as though no one had rung. I remember it ringing eight times in one shift and not one call was from a client. An even more bizarre thing happened one evening at the end of an episode of 'Roseanne'. The phone rang and I answered, and all I could hear was a beep. I found out through Telecom it is the beep you get when you ring your own phone number. When I got home that night there was one message on my answering machine: I played it and all I could hear was Roseanne's laughter. It was exactly the segment on the program that was screening when I'd picked up the receiver and put it down. How my number was rung I will never know—logically it's impossible. That really scared me. It was all right when we were all together at the Apple, but at home it was terrifying. I told Liz later I wanted no part of it again.

Probably the most incredible incident I can recall involved Liz putting a lipstick by a mirror. We all left the room, waiting for a message to be written on the glass. Three times we went back in. Nothing. We were losing interest but on the fourth attempt there was a message on the mirror. An arrow and heart had been written across the name 'Liz', all written without a break. It was blood-curdling stuff. There have been benefits, though: I'm now much more open and It has made me far more comfortable with death. I now know there is something out there, that I just won't disappear into the earth when I die—that there is a soul.

Another of Liz's friends, Tereza, is a vivacious woman of 25 who works in a Canberra photo laboratory. She admits openly she is both scared and sceptical about the events surrounding Liz. She was in the police station with another friend when a gold-coloured screw fell from the ceiling and began to ricochet across the room while Liz was giving evidence about an assault. She said there was no way of explaining the appearance of the screw: it just didn't compute. She went on to say that there had been a number of strange incidents connected with Liz that she could not explain.

One occurred when Tereza bought a new phone-answering machine. She took little notice when Liz told her Marty didn't like answering machines. Later, the pair went for a drive in Liz's Capri. During the spin Liz was annoyed because a song on one of her cassette tapes had been erased. And when they returned Tereza found all the messages on her answering machine that she had not erased, including her own taped response, had disappeared. On another occasion Tereza was talking to Liz on the phone and was 'getting cranky' about her friend's obsessive fascination with Marty. She told Liz to give it a rest. Liz retorted angrily, telling Tereza to take her unseen friends seriously. At that moment a vase filled with artificial flowers, which had been placed atop a three-tier table two-and-a-half years earlier, fell and smashed. Tereza said the experience terrified her because there was no window open and no wind. She had no explanation why that vase fell off that shelf at that very moment.

Tereza's Ford Laser has also been subject of strange electrical goings-on. The interior light had blown, and when it had been examined a break in the element could clearly be seen. As expected, when Tereza opened the door of her car the light didn't work—except when she parked outside Liz's house. Tereza said it was so spooky because it worked every time she parked outside her friend's house, yet nowhere else. 'It scares me, really scares me,' she complained. 'However, when I was in Liz's bedroom about 12 months ago she asked me if I could see Marty. I was not straining and I still don't know whether it was in my mind or not, but I saw an outline of an arm.' Tereza is convinced Liz also has the power of healing. She once hurt her hand while riding. She told Liz it wasn't broken, but it was swollen and extremely painful and she was going to get it X-rayed. Liz persuaded her to lie down in a dark room and within 15 minutes the swelling and the pain had disappeared.

Tereza suffered from leukaemia. Her white cell count was very high, requiring close monitoring by doctors. The unbalanced blood caused her to lose weight and periodically faint. Yet in mid-1994, after one 'healing' from Liz, Tereza's condition changed. She put on weight and her doctor, surprised by the dramatic improvement, ordered a blood test. It was normal. Her doctor thought a mistake had been made, so ordered another test. Again, it was normal. Although the healing didn't prove permanent, Tereza believes Liz has genuine healing power. She says Liz is the most unusual person she's met. 'You know exactly where you are with Liz,' she said. 'I liked her straight away because there is no bullshit and never a dull moment. And I can tell you she's not crazy!' Tereza pointed out that she herself was not psychic and, indeed, had no interest in the subject before she met Liz.

In April 1994 former Canberra policeman Steve Kirby was interviewing Liz at Erindale Police Station, following an assault on Liz by a client. Liz insisted her spirits were present. During the interview a gold-coloured screw fell from the roof onto Senior Constable Kirby's head. With the conservatism often associated with his job, Steve told me, 'I simply couldn't determine where the screw came from. It was a bit of a mystery.'

Another to experience the antics of Liz's spirit forces was David, a Canberra social worker. David had cause to visit Liz on a number of occasions—in his professional capacity—after Liz had been bashed by a former client. A 36-year-old with a healthy scepticism about anything unusual, David said he was completely mystified following the appearance from 'mid-air' of the hard-working potatoes. 'On my first visit to Liz, in August 1994, nothing happened, even though Liz insisted that I listen to her "spirit tapes" and turned off the light to demonstrate the presence of her "friends",' he told me.

> However, on my second visit I saw a paper clip fly off the kitchen table without any obvious assistance. Next, a potato flew onto a bench and dropped onto the floor from the direction of the curtain. I thought it was a trick and looked to see where the potato had been strung from the curtain, but I couldn't find any evidence. Liz had a friend with her and from then on I watched them both like a hawk. Sure enough, another two potatoes flew into the air and I thought to myself, 'Shit—these two are good.' Then I walked down the corridor and saw a pot plant move. And when I sat on Liz's bed I felt someone or something touch me on the back. It wasn't the two girls: they weren't anywhere near me. The incident didn't scare me, but I can't explain what happened.

In late December 1994 I caught up with Liz's mother. Although she does not approve of her daughter's work, she does recognise Liz's psychic gifts, which she believes have been passed down through several generations. Liz's great-grandmother, who was born in 1865 near Hamilton in Victoria, had the gift of precognition. She even accurately predicted the death of her own daughter, at the time an apparently healthy mother aged 29. Great-grandmother's son was witness to the bizarre prediction that his sister was soon to die. Precognition was but one of great-grandmother's gifts. A talent for water divining saw her in constant demand among the local farmers and, according to Liz's mother, she was very accurate. Liz's mother said her psychic connection was not as pronounced as her grandmother's, although she invariably knew when Liz was having problems. 'I always ring her up straight away to see if I can help,' she said.

Liz's mother also gave an example of Liz's healing abilities. Liz's mum suffers from excruciating headaches, the result of a botched operation performed in January 1994. 'By April [that year] I was nearly insane with pain and thought I'd go mad unless I got relief,' she said.

> The first time, Liz somehow knew I was suffering this intense pain and rang me. She said simply, 'I'll send Marty down to help you.' I was so desperate all I could say was, 'Oh God, I need something.' The pain was so terrible, yet about midnight I heard a voice I had never heard before calling my name. Soon after, I seemed to feel better and then, as though by magic, the headache and pain had gone. I went off to sleep and didn't wake till 8 am—and I'm always awake at 5. It was just unbelievable, and when Liz rang me next morning she was very relieved. I suffered another bout two weeks later. The pain was terrifying and I hadn't been able to eat much. Liz said, 'I'll send you some help' and the voices were there in the kitchen again. I heard them repeat three times, 'You must eat, you've got to eat.' I followed their instructions and ate some yoghurt. The pain went, and I slept soundly all night. I can't tell you how relieved I was—I'd been almost out of my mind. Mind you, all the doctors tell me at the pain clinic is to take all the painkillers, but they were making me so sick. So now if I'm in pain I ring Liz. It doesn't always work but most of the time it does.

[An incredible coincidence occurred two days after the second 'healing': there was a spirit message on Liz's tape recorder saying, 'How's [mother's name]?']

In late 1994 Liz was having her Ford Capri serviced at Gregory Ford in the Canberra suburb of Mitchell. While she waited she was chatting to Gregory's Service Adviser, Wendy, a down-to-earth woman in her late thirties and with two children. Wendy spends most of her working life dealing with the practical problems associated with car ownership and, at times, dissatisfied customers. She has little interest in the paranormal and describes herself as a 'fence-sitter'. Although, when two close relatives died, Wendy witnessed a stool 'falling over' for no reason and a small pile of washing left on a bed was found strewn on the floor. Yet on this particular afternoon as she spoke to Liz she saw a copy of *Women's Weekly* fly off the coffee table without any apparent physical assistance. Liz asked Wendy if she'd seen what happened and Wendy, somewhat startled, replied, 'I most certainly did.' I asked Wendy some months later if she had an explanation: 'I don't know how that *Women's Weekly* flew off that table because the office was totally enclosed, which discounted any possibility of wind or a draft,' she said. 'Liz told me at the time it was not unusual for things like that to happen. All I know is I saw it fly off and I don't have any explanation.'

The last extraordinary story involving Liz's witnesses took place one evening in early April 1995. At the end of a classic Canberra autumn day, I was feeling at peace with the world as I turned the key to the back door of my home. The phone rang, and I hurried to get it before the answering system clicked in; it was probably a work-related media inquiry, a common occurrence. Instead, it was Liz, excitedly telling me about something that sounded even more 'way out' than usual. I listened to her story, which involved a client. As I wandered around the loungeroom with the cordless phone I couldn't help but be conscious of my cynicism casting doubt on Liz's latest 'courtship of the spirits'. I was forced to take note, though, when she told me the events had just occurred and that the client was willing to discuss his experiences. I admired his courage because he didn't have a clue who I was or the reasons for my interest.

Ray, a 55-year-old construction worker, told me later that he occasionally eased his loneliness and sexual frustration by visiting prostitutes. He had driven his light truck up Liz's steep driveway at about 6.30 pm, secured the vehicle by pushing down the door locks, and slammed the driver's door shut. He cursed when he realised what he had done. (He told me during a second phone conversation, later in the evening, that Caressa was 'bloody good' at her job and maybe this had contributed to his carelessness—or he may have had something else on his mind.) Anyway, he'd locked his keys in the truck, something he'd done a dozen or so times since he bought it seven years ago. He wasn't overly worried because he knew how to open the door with a piece of wire or plastic tape: other people had tried unsuccessfully to do it but only Ray seemed to 'have the knack'. When he looked in the back of the truck, though, there was no suitable plastic or wire in sight. He didn't want to interrupt his session with Liz, so he just hoped that she might have something he could use to open the door later. Ray had put the key problem aside by the time he knocked on Liz's door. She welcomed the nervous, rotund construction worker and showed him to her bedroom. After they had sorted out the financial side of things—$100 for about three-quarters of an hour—they both heard banging on the walls outside the bedroom. Liz told him not to worry: it was just her spirit friends playing tricks. Ray recalls mentally 'sending her up' although he didn't say anything disparaging to her. In retrospect, he still doesn't have a clue what might have caused the banging. He said it sounded as though someone was walking around the house, deliberately thumping on the walls. As he undressed Ray told Liz he had locked his keys in the truck and wondered if she had the right type of plastic tape or wire to open the door. Liz suggested a coathanger, but Ray said it wouldn't work. As he continued disrobing the walls were still being thumped, so Ray decided to play the game with Liz: 'I tell you what, why don't you get your spirit friends to get my bunch of keys out of the truck,' he said sarcastically. 'In reality I thought the whole thing was absolute bullshit and all this spirit nonsense would spoil the sex.' Caressa replied that she would ask but could make no promises. 'Next thing I knew she had pissed off and left me starkers in the bedroom. I could hear voices and wondered what the hell was going on.'

Ray is a person who speaks little, despite his inquiring mind. A large man with strong, brawny hands calloused from years of work in the construction industry, he leads an uncomplicated existence and is happy to accept life as it comes. He prefers the satisfaction that comes from a day of hard physical work and feels most comfortable having a few beers with his mates after work.

His pleasures, in the main, are simple. But, having watched 'exposés' about spirit phenomena on television and having formed his own opinions, all he could think about Caressa was, 'Not another one.' 'I thought she was stuffed in the head,' he admitted later. 'She can talk at 1000 miles an hour and you can't get a word in edgeways.' Ray recalled her appearing edgy that night, and it was only after I told him Liz had been expecting another client shortly after him that he realised why. Liz wouldn't want another man hanging around the house: 'Men get nervous about other men—they think they might get harassed, bashed or blackmailed,' she explained.

Ray did not know then that Liz had a friend in the house to take phone calls and keep her company. Liz, in the meantime, had panicked, left Ray in his birthday suit, and rushed out to discuss with her receptionist to get rid of him before the next client arrived. The last thing she wanted was an immovable builder's truck in her yard and a 'satisfied client' in her lounge. She found the receptionist outside the front door, smoking a cigarette. She could not understand Liz's panic and recalled her pleading to 'Matt'—'Please, please get the keys out of the truck.' The receptionist tried to calm Liz down and said Ray could call the NRMA when he had finished.

Liz continued pleading for Matt to do something. The receptionist told me later that night that, not being particularly worried about the keys locked in the truck, she spent the time Ray was having sex with Liz smoking and taking a couple of phone calls. When I quizzed her again, a month later, she stressed that at no time did Liz call anyone on the phone or speak to a neighbour or friend to get help with opening the door of Ray's truck.

When Liz realised there was nothing else she could do she returned to the bedroom and poor Ray, who had been left to his own devices, wondering what the hell was going on. 'It was probably less than five minutes, but it seemed longer,' he said.

Caressa gabbled something about talking to her spirit friends about my keys. I remember looking at her and saying, 'Oh yeah?'—I was getting jack of the whole bloody thing. I must mention, though, you can usually tell when people are lying ... you get a feeling. But I thought she was telling the truth, or at least she believed what she was saying. When she started getting undressed other things came to mind and I completely forgot about the keys. She is a real 'pro'. She really knows how to get a guy aroused and, as usual, I was very satisfied. Then we moved to the bathroom for a shower. Caressa opened the door—I was following directly behind her when I saw what appeared to be a set of keys thrown on the floor near her feet. She picked up the keys and said to me, 'Jesus Christ! Look, are they your keys?' Well, I can tell you, I had the shock of my life: they were my keys. You could have knocked me down with a feather. There was no way those keys could have got inside the house. At the time I thought it was impossible. On the other hand, 'Caressa' was jumping up and down shouting about the power of her spirit friends and all she wanted to do was to ring you about the appearance of the keys. And then the banging started again, except this time it appeared to come from the roof and it didn't sound like cats.

Within five minutes of all this Liz spoke to me and then handed the phone to Ray. He appeared close to speechless. I asked him for a description of events but emphasised I did not want his name, for obvious reasons. He wasn't concerned about the 'Privacy Act' and surprised me by giving me not only his proper name but also his home and mobile phone numbers. I gave him my home phone number and told him he could ring me later that night if he wanted to talk.

Around 9 pm Ray rang me: 'Guess what? When I went out to the truck Caressa's 'friends' had removed a trowel from a bucket in the back of the truck and placed it on the bonnet. I can tell you, I had a few beers when I got home tonight.' He also mentioned Liz showing him spirit writing on the fridge, which apparently said, 'Good boy now.'

After Ray told me about the writing I called Liz, raced out, jumped on my Triumph, camera in hand, and flew to her house before the writing disappeared. (Spirit writing on her fridge seems to appear and disappear without warning or reason). As I walked up the driveway I noticed a couple of items that seemed rather odd. For starters, a wheeled garbage bin was jammed behind the receptionist's car and a shovel was leaning against Liz's front door. I spoke initially to the receptionist and soon after an excited, semi-clad Liz sprung out of the bedroom, having expedited a client to climax. Both Liz and the receptionist seemed perplexed by the bin and the shovel. Did someone place them there, or did the spirit forces move them? They didn't have a clue and nor did I. What I did know, though, was that the spirits were active that night, so the 'psychic solution' could not be dismissed!

Unfortunately, the spirit writing had disappeared. (Liz tells me that unless she stays in the kitchen watching the fridge the writing usually goes.) Meanwhile, Liz dashed back to the bedroom and, since I didn't want the client to catch me in the house with a camera, I went out the back door to chat with the receptionist, only to be confronted by another amazing scene. Liz's cats were eating what appeared to be freshly cooked pork, complete with crackling. The receptionist said there had been no meat in the house, so where had the meat come from? Had it been spiked with poison by a vindictive neighbour? Liz rang me later because she was terrified the cats might die. As it turned out, they remained healthy, but still she had no idea how the hot pork came to be in the backyard. It seems ludicrous to suggest her spirit friends put it there. Yet I had seen sweets manifest themselves, and Liz swore that other items of food had appeared previously. Another strange night.

I jumped back on the Triumph and rode home, wondering how could I come to terms with what had gone on. I had no idea. I decided to let a month go by, so that Ray might be able to speak more objectively about his experience. On 4 May I rang him, but he still had no logical explanation, in spite of discussing the incident with his son and another friend. There were, however, a couple of other things that had happened that night and that further unsettled him, and he agreed to meet me. I arranged to meet him at his home the following Monday night.

At our meeting Ray showed me his truck. Apart from the trowel, he had also found the imprint of a huge left hand on the bonnet after his visit to Liz. Ray has large hands, but he said that hand must have been fifty per cent larger than his; it also appeared clawed or malformed: 'It was as though the left arm had stretched across the bonnet of the truck, allowing the right hand to place the trowel in front of the windscreen,' he explained.

> Not only did the hand imprint puzzle me, but I found a serrated knife in the back of the truck and scratch marks on the driver's door. The scratches were identical to the high points on the serrated knife. I hadn't seen that knife before and didn't have a clue where it came from. And I also noticed the moulding rubber around the door had been cut, although that might have been done previously. I got shivers up my spine—it was a really crawly feeling thinking about what might have gone on.
>
> My son and friends reckoned it was set-up job. They reckoned Caressa had a 'friend' who opened the truck and put the keys on the floor outside her bedroom. More to the point, they asked me what I had been drinking that night, yet I hadn't had a drop before visiting Caressa. I've thought about it all many times. I now know Caressa had a friend in the house, so it's possible she could have opened the truck door, although I doubt whether she would've had the knack. If the NRMA had been called they would have wanted my membership card and I'm not a member. She could have called a neighbour or friend. But if they had succeeded how could they throw the keys on the floor without being heard or seen? The door between the lounge room and the passageway to the bedroom was closed and there was no one there. I've not only spent many hours discussing this—I've even tried to simulate the 'dropping of the keys' from door knobs in my own place. It doesn't

work: the keys were virtually thrown through the door line; if they'd been on the knob they would have dropped behind the door when it was opened.

More easily explained was the trowel being taken from the bucket of tools and put on the bonnet. But why go to the trouble? I don't like dabbling in this sort of thing. Ghosts don't remove keys and put them somewhere else ... they don't pick up trowels from the back of trucks and put them on bonnets. What explanation is there? I think Caressa is telling the truth, although I think she's slightly mad.

Ray is not alone in thinking this. Liz has been ridiculed for her belief in the spirit world, even by her close friends.

I really don't know what happened that night. Part of me says it's a set-up job and I was tricked or conned, the other part says there is no logical explanation, but how could it be done'?

Liz put her side of the argument, saying her friend wouldn't have any idea how to break into a truck and, besides, her neighbours won't talk to her because she's a hooker. She admits a friend could have been contacted in time and opened the door, but says she doesn't know anyone who could break into a vehicle. In any case, there wasn't enough time, and why go to all that trouble when it wasn't her problem?

I visited Liz on the night of 17 May to clarify aspects of the story. I was interested to know if she recognised the knife Ray had given to me. Sure enough, when she opened the cutlery drawer there was a spoon from the same set. This only deepened the mystery. If her friend, or an accomplice, say, had broken into the truck with the knife surely they would have put the nearly new knife back in the kitchen—why throw it in the back of the truck?

In my final interview with Ray, in late 1995, he did concede that the knife might have been used to open the truck. But he told me he had tried to do it with a similar knife and had failed: 'It just wasn't the right shape to prise open the button lock,' he said.

One thing I can tell you is I'm not going to forget the experience in a hurry—in fact, never! Why would someone who had opened the truck and thrown the keys on the floor in front of the bedroom bother to lock the truck again? Because I found the truck still locked when I went to go. It just doesn't make sense. I often think about that night and, to be honest, I have no explanation. I wish I did.

My last 'witness' was a discarnate spirit that came through Canberra medium Monica Hamers during a trance reading in August 1995. In my opinion the reading is of interest: as we are dealing with phenomena even the most broad-minded scientist would have difficulty accepting. In the past I had used Monica's guides to answer difficult questions. A number of entities regularly spoke through her and I became so familiar with the 'personalities' that I could usually identify them within seconds. I thought it would be interesting to see if Monica could help again. I first asked the entity whether it was important to include here details of the more degrading side of prostitution. The entity, whom I could not recognise from previous readings, responded,

> It is important to tell the whole story and this includes the sexual side; it is part of the story. Is it truth that you ate a pleasant Christmas dinner; then is it truth that nothing happened or is it truth that you eventually excreted it in a less pleasant state? The truth is that we have to cover humanity from the highest to the lowest, that always baser things attract the most horror in people. But they remember them: they attract attention because they are more dramatic and vivid.

> While it is true there are angels who create beauty there are also demons which create filth. It is a fact about humanness that the good and the bad are so closely interrelated. For example, the design of the human body is such that the organs of excretion are parallel with the organs of pleasure: one goes with the other. This applies also to the work you are trying to do with the prostitute. Without the sexual act, there would be no procreation and

> yet it has been used for the baser side instead of the spiritual: this again is human nature But, looking at the human body, for example, how could you understand sickness and disease if you do not understand the functioning of elimination? It is very easy to understand the functioning of your mouth or a woman's breasts or other organs of pleasure that create attraction and outer beauty, yet without the operation of other less pleasant parts of your body—the bowels and anus—these things would die and not be able to function. This applies to life too. The spiritual being who functions within you and is close to God and is able to raise itself to exalted heights of awareness is living within a physical body that can also lower itself to states of depravity. What you have written is truth, that there is an unpleasant side to all things. While it may be not pleasant it is the truth.

I followed up my first question by asking whether I had been fooled at any time or whether what I had perceived to be true was in fact true. The answer:

> The earthbound spirits around this woman are genuine; the states in which they are being suspended is genuine. It is cosmic truth that like attracts like. These males were strongly influenced by their sexuality before they died and have been attracted by the energy this woman emits. Sexual energy is very powerful and the transmissions from her solar plexus give them energy on which they can feed. Poltergeist activity is the transmission of energy from the lower frequencies to the earth plane, which enables phenomenas to occur that do not appear to have a physical form. In fact, the physical forms are of a baser energy; they are not visible to you but they still have movement. If they are able to achieve, for example, the throwing of a stone or rolling of an egg there is a still a 'hand' behind it that creates the phenomenon, but the hand itself is not of this frequency.

I asked the entity whether on the nights when the greatest activity took place it was a combination of the three discarnate spirits or the work of one particular spirit. The entity replied that it was a combination of all three energies but that in particular there was a spirit from a child present: 'The child was brought to the house for release from its earthbound state and was able to give much energy because there was no preconceived awareness.'

Whether you accept the entity's explanation or not, it does give another fascinating perspective to this intriguing story. Another thing that interested me, after sifting through the witnesses' evidence, was that most of the witnesses did not know each other—Liz was the common thread. There were other names Liz gave me, one of them a soldier who met Liz at a Canberra nightclub. He was not aware she was a prostitute, but when he 'came the heavy' back at her house he soon lost interest as objects started flying through the air. Maybe it's nice to have a poltergeist as a 'friend'.

9
Amazing happenings at Humpty Doo

Late in 1998 I spent two months relieving in the busy Northern Command public affairs office in Darwin. I took the short-term posting with some reluctance: Canberra's spring weather was gorgeous, in contrast with the hot, oppressive conditions that prevail during the build-up to the wet season in the north. Yet, as so often happens, there was a very good reason for my 'northern exposure'. It seemed that some external agency was sowing seeds in my subconscious and guiding me on to my next case. Yes, the job in Darwin was demanding, but there was sufficient spare time to research one of Australia's most amazing poltergeist cases, certainly the most bizarre case I have investigated. More importantly what had gone on at Humpty Doo lent further credibility to my Canberra findings.

On the four-hour flight from Sydney to Darwin I had time to think about a recent bike ride with a couple of Air Force friends to watch mighty Mick Doohan win the 500 cc World Championship at Phillip Island in Victoria. It was early October and, although the weather had been indifferent, the trip was superb and we looked forward to a summer of great riding. So much for that idea! I later wondered whether Liz's poltergeist was associated with the goings-on in Humpty Doo. In Canberra two gold-coloured rocks had been placed in precise positions on my Triumph Trident, the throttle was jammed open, and the mirrors were pushed inwards at exactly the same angle. In the Humpty Doo case a precise, 70-centimetre Trident symbol made with river pebbles mysteriously appeared in the most alien of circumstances. It sounds ludicrous to suggest a connection but it could not be discounted.

I landed at Darwin around 2 pm on Armistice Day—surely a good omen. But my enthusiasm quickly dissipated as I walked out of the airport lounge and into sauna-like temperatures. It was 35°C with more than 90 per cent humidity. When I left my house in Canberra at 5.15 am it had been −2°C, with frost on the ground. Out of the taxi window in steamy Darwin, past the blossoming frangipani, all I could see were 'mad' golfers pottering around in shorts beneath giant silver sun umbrellas Idly, I queried the driver, 'Any good ghost stories in Darwin lately?' He became very animated and told me what he'd heard about the strange happenings at Humpty Doo. For the remainder of the short journey to the RAAF base I was regaled with the outrageous stories that had filled the local press earlier in the year.

I later found out that the truth was even more bizarre than I first imagined. That made me wonder about other strange stories I read in the *Northern Territory News*, including what happened to a Darwin man who tried to capture an angry, deadly king brown snake when drunk. His heart stopped three times, he spent seven weeks in a coma, and finally his left arm had to be amputated just below the shoulder. The same paper also ran a story about a terrified firefighter who claimed he ran over an 'apparition' of a woman. The incident occurred on a gravel road about 22 kilometres from Adelaide River during a 'hell of a storm'. 'I felt no thump but I thought I'd killed her,' he told reporter Ross Irby. He stopped his truck but could find no body or blood on it: 'I don't believe in ghosts or spiritual stuff but there was definitely someone there—the hair was standing on end when I told the story to the missus,' he said to Irby. Two other residents, a father and daughter, have also seen the forlorn woman, the daughter 'running over' the woman too. Spooks and ghosts were alive in the north!

The locals call 'the wet' the 'suicide season' and my taxi driver informed me that this year's build-up to the wet was one of the worst in years. Cyclone Thelma, one of the most savage cyclones on record, appeared off the Darwin coast. It battered the Tiwi Islands to the north with wind speeds reaching 320 kph, but thankfully in Darwin the winds reached only 100 kph and its clouds dumped a mere 1300 millimetres of rain in four days. Thelma finally moved west towards the Kimberley coast and petered out into a rain depression. But Darwin did have its positives: when I was asked by a delightful young lady to come around for a spa, heated water wasn't required ... nor were togs. Darwin was not dull.

The way stories develop amazes me. I was playing golf at Darwin Golf Club, in the usual torrid conditions, with locals John and Barbara Stacey when I asked if they were familiar with the Humpty Doo story. Barbara immediately responded and gave me the name of Jack Ellis, editor of the *Litchfield Times*. He was the journalist who broke the story, which then spread like wildfire: a news crew from Channel 7's 'Today Tonight' program even flew to Darwin to whip up the story.

* * *

Why include this story from the Top End in the biography of a Canberra prostitute? I had three main reasons.

First, I wanted another story with characters that were uniquely Australian. Carl Gustav Jung could not be more remote from the average Australian, but the characters involved in the Humpty Doo case you could meet in a country pub.

Second, you could not get more different circumstances: a prostitute working from a suburban house in sedate Canberra and five people, from very different backgrounds, living in a house in Darwin's primary mango-growing area.

Third, many of the happenings, in such different circumstances, are remarkably similar: writing on the walls, objects being thrown, apparent dematerialisation and rematerialisation of objects, and, most importantly, in both cases the energy seeming to emanate from an 'intelligent' source. For example, when the ABC first turned up with news cameras, scrabble pieces left deliberately on the bathroom floor by the residents for the 'spirit intelligence' spelt out NO CAMERAS. One of the female residents said the 'intelligence', or 'it', appeared to know what the tenants were thinking and certainly responded to actions. Again, when she spoke to the reporter from 'Today Tonight' the scrabble pieces spelt out NO TV. Further, in both Humpty Doo and Canberra the force seemed to draw strength from stormy, humid conditions.

I believe parallels can be drawn, and I went to great lengths to document the observations of reliable witnesses in the Darwin story, as I did with those in Canberra. Like some Darwin residents, I am often the butt of friends' jokes, friends who simply cannot accept what I say I have seen. In my opinion, both cases present overwhelming evidence, yet there will still be some who are not prepared to accept the personal experiences of so many reliable witnesses.

* * *

My investigations started when I finally caught up with Jack Ellis. A former Sergeant Radio Technician in the RAAF and now editor of the *Litchfield Times*, Jack is a bright, likeable person with an impish sense of humour. He also has a larrikin streak, which may help him as a newspaper editor but probably curtailed his service career. It was the end of the week, Jack told me, and the house that was the subject of rumours was only a few kilometres from his office, so, prompted by a tip-off from a staff member, Jack decided to go and check out 90 McMinns Drive. It was Friday 27 March 1998. 'First of all I thought someone was setting us up for an April Fools Day joke: we'd pulled a few ourselves in the local region,' Jack admitted.

The paper was due to come out on April 2 and we were

running an April Fools story in that issue. I thought, 'Sure as eggs someone is setting us up' and my inclination was to do nothing, but eventually curiosity got the better of me. When I got to the house, there were Dave Clark, Jill Sommerville and Kirsty Agius sitting around in the kitchen and I've got to tell you I was sceptical. I really didn't believe in this stuff, but I was curious. It was a long kitchen and I deliberately put myself up against the wall so that no one could do anything around me without me seeing. From this position I could see all three occupants, the window and the doorways. The three of them were telling me about these objects flying about, even when visitors were around. I remember thinking to myself 'Well, it isn't happening here. That's for bloody sure!'

At about that stage there was a rattling on the fan above my head and this shower of gravel appeared. Some landed on me. It was almost as though they were falling 'through' the fan. Kirsty cried out excitedly, 'Here it is. See! See! We told you, we told you!' I wasn't convinced and jumped up and looked out the window but there was no one there. I doubled-checked the doorway, all the rooms—even the ceiling, which was solid—and there was certainly no one else in the house. We chatted some more then there was an almighty thump in the middle of the house.

Off we went into Dave and Jill's bedroom and I could see their mattress and sheets had been thrown about. They told me their room had been neat and tidy, yet here was the mattress upside down and sheets flung against the wall. I was a bit suss about that one because it could have been set up. I went to take pictures of a window smashed by flying objects when another shower of gravel game down and hit me. That was pretty spooky, and I said to myself, 'Sure as heck there's something funny going on in here.' I finished the interview and walked out to the car: I remember being really nervous walking from the house to the car, thinking 'This is bloody ridiculous, I don't believe in this stuff.' But I was quite edgy, waiting for something to happen.

And that started the whole media saga. I was there on numerous occasions, including the night they packed up to leave. On that final evening we were in the bar ... it would have been about 8 pm on Friday 15 May. We were just standing around and there was another shower of gravel on the roof and over the cars, including Jill's, which was parked under an awning. Heaps of people were there; it would have been nearly impossible to set the thing up. The sceptics reckoned the residents were putting rocks on the top of the fans and then starting them up. I tried it at home on one of my ceiling fans to see what would happen. The trajectory of the rocks was totally different—they were just flung against the wall.

It was not the people in the house, of that I'm positive. Maybe it could have been done with special effects, but it would cost a lot of money and a substantial amount of time and effort. There's no logic behind that explanation because, in the end, these people were ducking publicity, not seeking it. To be honest, I've run out of explanations.

I put it to Jack that surely he had a commercial interest in the story because it ran over several weeks? He agreed that his circulation did increase 10 to 15 per cent but 'Realistically it didn't create a huge financial gain.'

The five people who lived at 90 McMinns Drive, a basic four-bedroom fibro house built in 1972, made an interesting group. The lease had been taken out in August 1997 by Dave Clark and his partner Jill Sommerville, a likeable couple in their mid-thirties. Dave, a Harley-riding mechanic who feels most comfortable in stubbies, T-shirt and thongs, proved to be an astute observer of the goings-on. His down-to-earth approach to life and his dry sense of humour were at odds with Jill's nature. Jill talks with a rapid-fire, nervous intensity and has a far more serious approach to life. The house they had rented was on about 2 hectares of land; it was surrounded by mango trees and vehicles and protected by a high cyclone fence. (When I interviewed them, they had moved into their new rented property a few kilometres from McMinns Drive.)

To ease the burden of the $250-a-week rent and to help out Kirsty Agius (a close friend of Jill), her husband Andrew (a strapping driller who prefers an itinerant life in the bush life to domesticity) and their baby Jasmin with accommodation, Dave and Jill offered the others a room in mid-February 1998. Kirsty, Brisbane born, in her early thirties, and tall and slender with intense brown eyes, was the only one of the group who had previously experienced unusual phenomena. Two years earlier at Bachelor, a township named after a wartime airfield, Kirsty and Andrew had had stones thrown through their front door with great force. They concluded that children were responsible, but they saw no one. And, during employment as a camp cook on a drilling rig in outback New South Wales, Kirsty had seen coffee cups rattling for no apparent reason. These things gave strength to the theory that Kirsty might be attracting the forces. She wondered, too, and was relieved when the activity did not follow her when she finally moved 100 kilometres away to a house in Adelaide River.

Gavin Murphy, a tattooed, brawny fisherman who lives life at full throttle, including wrenching the guts out of his long-suffering, unsilenced Kawasaki 900, moved in a few days later. Sunburnt and with powerful shoulders, Murph was not known for his patience and amazed the others by not thumping some of the media who believed the whole thing was a hoax.

It is important to note that none of the residents had any particular religious or spiritual beliefs and none could recall any experience, such as using ouija boards, that might have encouraged the phenomena.

Sydney Morning Herald features writer Frank Robson was one of the many reporters who covered the story and the residents consider that he wrote the most objective report of what had been taking place. Kirsty gave me a copy of his magazine article and when I returned to Canberra I phoned Frank to congratulate him on his balanced coverage. Frank's evidence was important and he kindly agreed to his material being used in this chapter. We talked about the Canberra and Humpty Doo cases and I quickly realised he faced the same problem as I did: the lack of credibility. 'I've given up trying to describe the Humpty Doo experience to friends,' said Frank. Similarly, he told me one of Darwin's ABC reporters, Tracy Farrer, had said to him,: 'I'll never forget it, but the [mockery] reached a stage where I simply buttoned up.' Paranormal researcher Paul Cropper rang Frank for a chat and admitted, 'I thought I'd enjoy telling people, but it's just too hard.' I knew how they felt because I've been the butt of many a joke from friends and colleagues, especially those in the military.

Robson's initial exposure was not dissimilar to Jack Ellis's and he set the scene with suitable colour in *Good Weekend* magazine on 13 June 1998:

> Behind the nondescript blue house is a small home bar made of corrugated iron. It is decorated with booze labels, pictures of motorbikes, an Australian flag, and a display of girlie shots the tenants called the 'tit board'. Not long ago, a tenant called Kirsty Agius began adding pictures of large penises (from *Womens Forum*), generating fierce dispute with the boys. The conflict surfaces briefly on my first night at the house, when four of us sit at the bar drinking beer. 'Bloody dicks everywhere,' grumbles tenant Dave Clark. 'I can't get used to them.' Kirsty Agius turns to me, 'Typical,' she says. 'They're upset about a few dicks, but look at all the tits up there!' Clark: 'No, no Kirsty. You can't compare dicks and tits. A dick is …'

And then Frank describes his first experience: eight or ten pebbles appear from above their heads and hit the bar top with a rattle, that is much louder than one would expect. Frank's observation is that the pebbles descended gently, which is similar to my observation in Liz's bedroom, when the cigarette lighter drifted slowly across the room. In both cases the laws of gravity appeared to be defied. So, here we have the first interesting parallels. Sex, an increased noise level, 'slow' movements, and objects apparently appearing from nowhere. Later, witnesses spoke of objects moving with 'lightning speed and force'—again as in my experience at Liz's place.

My research into other cases leads me to conclude that sex, or even the discussion of it, can raise the energy necessary to increase the chance of phenomena. So can oppressive heat and storms.

This appears to be the case at Humpty Doo. The three months of disruption began in late January, in the middle of the wet season, and Darwin was experiencing spectacular lightning displays. It was also three weeks after Kirsty had joined the household. Initially, rocks were being thrown indiscriminately around the yard; the residents suspected kids armed with catapults. But one night the formula changed. While the tenants were sitting in the lounge room with the sliding door open rocks suddenly came smashing through the doorway into the house. According to Dave, the rock throwing went on for three nights. But they found nothing: 'I was really getting pissed off. This was serious.' For once Dave's voice was raised.

> Finally I'd had a gutful. I went outside with a loaded 22 Sterling semi-automatic, ready to sort it out once and for all. I found nothing. We were all getting angry, so we prepared a plan to 'catch them'. It was a combined effort and the three of us shot out from different doorways to make sure we nabbed them. I even had my trailbike ready to chase them. We thought the kids were not only smart but bloody quick. Then we wondered what was really going on when rocks started falling out of the ceiling! Right, I thought, we'll shut all the bloody doors. The windows didn't matter as they were fly-screened. It didn't make any difference, rocks were still falling from nowhere and then cutlery started flying around the house.

Jill, chain smoking and still affected by the antics, interrupted Dave in his animated description of events and admitted that she'd been frightened. 'Some time later we found a piece of paper under a pot with a death threat written on it saying, "You will all die",' she nervously recalled. After the media filmed the note the same message appeared scribbled on a wall in the house with a felt pen. Even the film crews encouraged the tenants to call the police. 'I felt a little better when they arrived,' Jill conceded. 'They convinced us we were not the victims of local louts.' Dave pointed out, though, that the cops had glass thrown around their feet during their investigation. 'They were nervous,' he laughed, and with his laconic humour he described how the female cop went for her side-arm in true 'western style' when a rock crashed onto the roof.

> They didn't hang around. They pissed off in a hurry. Towards the end of our time in the house we even had a visit by a Chubb security guard who'd been hired by the owner to make sure nothing was being knocked off. He shot through mighty quick when a blunt knife was thrown near his feet as he was about to leave the house.

Dave might have been casual, but Jill's fear was understandable. During the height of 'its' activity, steak knives were thrown into walls with considerable force and a large knife was stuck into Murph's mattress. Canberra-based researcher, Tony Healy saw a large skinning knife fly less than a foot from his head: 'I found it almost impossible to see how anyone could have thrown it, especially as there was a real risk of injury. Kirsty's toddler Jasmin was in the kitchen with her mother when a heavy piece of glass hit the wall and ricocheted across the floor near Jasmin. No mother is going to do that!'

The poltergeist took little notice of the police or anyone else. During the ensuing months every resident suffered, at various times, at the hands of the 'mischievous' entity referred to by the residents as 'it' or 'the fucking thing'. By the time the residents moved out, more than 40 people—priests, journalists, cameramen, tradespeople, teachers, security staff ... you name it—had witnessed inexplicable events at the house.

But all this might have been restricted to the residents' 'tall-tale' series until one Saturday evening, when 'it' went right off. Twelve hours of madness made the residents realise they were dealing with an unpredictable, unknown, unseen and potentially dangerous force. Objects were continually thrown; windows and furniture were smashed with incredible force. As the tenants cleaned up one room the next was being trashed, with glasses and other breakables smashed into tiny pieces. So it continued. To make matters worse, in Murph's bedroom, they found a 1-metre-long, geometrically perfect 'devil's trident' made of pebbles. Dave said it was so perfect it would have taken a person hours to piece together, yet it was probably formed in moments. The tenants were convinced the medieval symbol signified evil. No wonder the girls were in tears. They wanted to leave but couldn't because they had been drinking heavily.

Finally, they found enough Dutch courage to take 'it' on: 'Fuck you, ghost; we're staying,' they yelled. Still jumpy, they went to bed. But the scratching and knocking on the walls got louder, said Kirsty: 'We all had our lights on and weren't game to go outside and see what was happening. Finally, it eased off but when we got up in the morning, tired and cranky after a terrible night's sleep, it started again.'

Jill said the only reason they didn't move out the following day was the owners were on holiday in Queensland.:

> We wanted our bond money so we could move into another house. None of us are rich—we were stuck. We were even more pissed off when we walked outside and found stones covering the cars and the bar. We didn't know what to do, so in desperation we rang a phone-in clairvoyant in Sydney who advised us to dip a crucifix in water, preferably holy water. We were told to touch each corner of every room in the house with the crucifix and then drink some of the water. Of course, we didn't have holy water, so Dave thought the next best thing was clean creek water and he nicked off to flooded section to gather supplies. In sounds crazy, but we were frantic and prepared to try anything. Amazingly, it did work for two days. Then

'it' came back. The clairvoyant had told us to get a priest if the holy water failed, so after three or four days Dave drove to Darwin and fetched Father Stephen de Souza, a Jesuit priest from St Mary's cathedral.

Father Stephen was the first of three priests who attempted to 'clear' the house. On his first visit he attempted to bind the spirit with prayer. He told Frank Robson that before he started he looked around the entire house. 'In the kitchen I noticed a microwave oven with a steak knife on top of it. As I walked away, one of the tenants called, "Father!" I turned and saw that steak knife flying straight at me. I saw that thing coming very fast and at about half a metre away—as though it had hit something—it fell at my feet.' Father Stephen took such events in his stride because in his native India, he'd been one of a number of priests involved in blessing demonised houses.

Personally, I was particularly interested in his witnessing a beer glass being smashed against a wall with a sound similar to a rifle shot. He said it sounded like a 100 glasses smashed and he dismissed the idea of a hoax: 'I have seen too much of this to waste my time with tricks,' he said. As I experienced with Liz, on three occasions objects appeared or were smashed, accompanied by a sound similar to that of the discharge of a large-calibre rifle. Regardless, the residents were thankful because on one of his visits Father Stephen managed to quieten the house for three days before bedlam erupted again.

Local Catholic priest Father Tom English, from the Church of St Francis of Assisi, was next. In spite of his efforts in blessing the house, he also witnessed things flying around and crashing into walls during his five visits. Understandably, Kirsty aired her concern about the safety of her baby, but Father Tom told her it was his belief that the mischievous entity would not harm the baby. Ironically, he thought, the baby might even think she was being entertained, whereas adults would be frightened. Kirsty was not so sure: during a period of intense activity the angry mum yelled out in frustration, 'You're too gutless to go into my room, you wimp.' But when she went into her bedroom (which had previously not been touched) an hour later everything was knocked off the dressing table. For Kirsty, the reaction to her 'challenge' and other incidents convinced her that 'it' was an intelligent, mischievous force.

Several other 'experts', among them a Sydney medium hired by the 'Today Tonight' show, tried to 'quieten' the house. Apparently this hired medium clears places of unwanted entities for up to $50 a room. He told reporter Max Anderson that he had successfully 'ghost-busted' a Woollahra brothel because what was happening there was affecting business. (This lends weight to the idea that intense sexual activity may attract poltergeist activity.) But he admitted that, in spite of using 'psychic seals' at Humpty Doo, he was uncertain of success and, later, that this was the most extreme case he had come across. He told Anderson that 'it' seemed to be connected with the energy of the earth and the local land: 'If that's the case there's nothing I can do. It also seems to have an intelligence, which means it could be very dangerous.'

The medium's doubts were proved valid. His efforts to clear the place were rewarded by renewed activity the following day. A Greek Orthodox priest then tried, setting up an altar, blessing each room, and reading passages from his large black book. 'It' was not impressed: it tried to wrench the book from his hands and finally attempted to twist his arm behind his back. Dave said that priest left and was never seen again. Even Murph decided God's word might help and jumped on his Kwaka to collect a bible from a Palmerston church. According to Dave, the priest tried to counsel Murph, but to no avail: all Murph wanted was 'God's book'. 'It' wasn't impressed and Murph found the Bible ripped up in his bedroom. Murph reasoned that if God wasn't the answer maybe bullets would suffice: He laid out a box of 44 Magnum bullets in his bedroom, but they either 'disappeared' or were found scattered around the house.

Kirsty spoke of a number of tricks, such as writing on the wall with a felt pen. It was mainly scribble 'but often the words were legible' she said. Even the felt pen appeared from nowhere: none of the occupants used or owned one.

> My husband Andrew spoke to Father Tom, asking him whether the herb sage would keep evil spirits away. Father Tom didn't know, but after he left I went into the shower and there, on the bathroom floor, were the letters 'MF', formed with pieces of our sage. We never found the sage bottle, nor did we find out what 'MF' meant. Murph would say something like 'bullbags' and then we would find 'bags' written in the hall.
>
> Father Tom claimed one of his female parishioners used to play there as a kid and that doors used to slam and other unusual things occurred, so maybe it just started off again. I know the bloody thing understood what we were thinking or saying. It never hurt us: it was as though it was playing a bloody game with us.

The tenants wondered whether all this activity may have been created by the restless spirits of a couple of Murph's mates, who were incinerated in a four-wheel drive three months earlier. They were driving home, drunk but only minutes from the house, when they smashed into a tree off the Stuart Highway. The truck was filled with paints and thinners—one or both of them earned a living as painters. It proved a lethal concoction. The truck simply exploded. They didn't stand a chance. Kirsty said the pair were just normal 'yahoo' young fellas who got on the booze. 'We tried to contact them with the Scrabble board pieces we left out on the bathroom floor,' she said.

> We checked names written on the walls or marked out with pebbles. Incredibly, the word 'fire' was laid out with texta pens that had been in my zipped-up suitcase, ready to be given as a present! 'Skin', 'car', 'help' and finally 'Trouy'—the name of one of the guys killed in the truck—were spelt out.

Trouy's mother heard about the Scrabble 'messages' and flew up from Adelaide because she wanted to communicate with her son. She was on her knees in the bathroom, writing a message—'Is that you, Trouy? It's Mum here, and everything's all right'—when a piece of glass fell through her hair onto the floor. Freelance cameraman Danny Sim, who witnessed the incident, reported Troy's mother describing the feeling as like 'fingers running through her hair'. Danny said the poor woman freaked out and broke down in tears: 'It was an emotional moment for all of us and really cut us up,' he told me. 'I admit I was close to tears. In my opinion it was impossible for someone to set it up.'

Ironically, the tenants queried the evidence because when Trouy was spelt on the floor with the Scrabble pieces it was T-R-O-Y. He'd been christened Trouy, but they knew he hated that: he always wanted his name spelt 'Troy'. Another unusual aspect of the incident was that the glass seemed to come from one of the shattered windows. Danny went out and retrieved a bit about the same size and then dropped it from roughly the same height as the mother's head. It splintered on the tiled floor, whereas the piece that ran through the mother's hair remained intact.

* * *

While Dave and Jill relaxed over a couple of beers in their new house they continued describing their experiences. Dave, ever the handyman, had a reasonably extensive array of tools, which he kept in a shed separate from the house. He said items—from spanners to vice-grips—that were housed in a toolbox would suddenly appear in the house or on the roof. 'I know it's crazy but they must have flown through the solid walls,' he said waving his hands.

> And the night 'it' went right off my stereo flew off its support. Now, to do that you'd have to drill a hole in the bathroom wall and stick your hand through and push it over. I thought, 'Fuck this,' and promptly packed it up. One afternoon we were having a few beers to cool down and that was the signal for the bottle opener to go mad, flying around, landing on the roof or around the bar. We were always losing it. Our bedroom was trashed up to five times a day—the mattress frequently jammed against the wall, sheets and cosmetics just thrown around the room. Now

> why would we do that, I ask you? Nothing moved or happened in the bedroom when we were there, and never in the three months did we see any object start to move. Although one day, out of the corner of my eye, I saw a CD picked up and thrown. Jill had the feeing something was watching us. And you can't blame the girls for being frightened when a message was written on the wall: 'You will die tonight.'

Dave, the memories still fresh in his mind, said in the end it got so bad that, in spite of the fact that they put every glass in closed cupboards, they would still appear from somewhere and smash with great force against the walls or windows.

> Even an empty plastic spirits bottle [as used by the airlines] blasted through the glass of a dining room cabinet with a noise similar to the discharge of rifle. The force was so great that it left a huge hole many times the diameter of the bottle. I also began to notice that when thunderstorms and lightning were around 'it' appeared to use this energy to do what it wanted. And when Murph revved up his Kawasaki 900 with open pipes or if I gave my unmuffled Harley a handful 'it' used to go 'ape' on the noise.

Towards the end, the tension between the five often resulted in heated arguments; this also seemed to create energy for increased activity. Even such an innocuous thing as Andrew reading the Psalms to create peace seemed to put the 'energy' into a 'frenzy'. Dave, meanwhile, was starting to take quite an interest in the poltergeist and came up with the interesting observation that there appeared to be a circle of energy in the house during its activity: 'Objects always seemed to fly clockwise and on the odd occasion be accompanied by an eerie cold wind,' he said. I had certainly witnessed cold winds during my research into other cases, but the clockwise energy was new. Most of the activity centred around the house, although a knife from the kitchen drawer once appeared in the swimming pool more than 50 metres away. At the time, Brett, a friend of Murph's, was in the pool. His mongrel dog, Ted, went 'ballistic' because the knife appeared to track his master around the pool, as though it was following him. When Brett finally noticed the errant knife it suddenly zeroed in. He leapt out of the pool and refused to go in again.

A number of other witnesses had their own stories to tell. Of particular interest is Irene Winter's account. She accepted the job of cleaning the house at the end of the dry season in 1997 and described the residence as 'spooky'. She said the inside of the house was cold. 'Doors kept shutting on their own, even though there was no breeze flowing through,' she said. 'I opened up the house because it was a lovely day outside, yet it was still freezing inside.' A carpet cleaner who arrived while Irene was there picked up the same vibes and promptly called out to Irene, 'I'm out of here' and left without touching a carpet. While Irene admitted, 'They paid me for five hours and I only did one because it was so freaky.' Irene's story leads one to think that the 'force' used to lie dormant, waiting for the right time to really strut its stuff.

Former resident of the house, local school teacher Annette Taylor, was one of the few who suffered physically at the hands of the entity. Annette, her partner Lloyd Green and their young son Zeke visited Dave and Jill when 'it' was at its most active. Annette was greeted with a shower of gravel and from that moment seemed targeted by other missiles, which always fell short of her body. Significantly, Annette saw things moving through the air, which she said, would hover and then speed up. On one occasion, as she was telling the group that things like that were well known in her Maori culture and could not hurt them, some of Dave's tools became airborne. A vice-grip headed towards Zeke's head and Annette instinctively put her hand up to protect her child. She recalled, 'It hit me hard on my wrist and my arm was swollen and purple for days afterwards. I got in the way, I think.' Annette recalled that when she lived in the house she was sure there was 'something' there: 'I used to say this to people, and they would look at me as though I was weird.'

To cap off Annette, Lloyd and Zeke's visit, there was another amazing incident. As Jill wandered off to the toilet she noticed a cross made of gravel on the carpeted passageway outside the bathroom. She called the others to look at the perfectly formed cross, which was about 35 centimetres long. Lloyd described it like this: 'Every pebble had been turned so that its flat side was on the outside edge of the cross and the corners were all perfectly butted up. Even if I'd sat there with a straight-edge, a square and a rule it would have taken me hours to make something so neat and perfect.' Dave agreed, recalling that it took his breath away when he first saw the cross because it was perfect. He intuitively felt the cross had amazing powers, yet it had been formed in only moments: there had been a regular procession to the toilet. Annette saw the cross and was taken aback, like all the others.

Jill told me Annette's other son had been killed in a road accident a month. One can only wonder whether Annette and Trouy's mother were being sent 'signs' from their sons. And when Dave picked up some of the pebbles from the formation a chain reaction of rock throwing around the house ensued, causing Zeke to wake and cry. The perfection of the cross reminded Dave that after one 'crazy night' pebbles were found on the bar table, laid out, like tiles, in perfect symmetry. 'It was hard to believe because they were perfectly formed, right to the edge of the table, yet there were none on the ground,' he said. This 'perfection' is in line with my experiences: although on a much smaller scale, the two gold-coloured rocks I found on my motorbike were placed exactly in the middle of the filler cap and rider's seat.

Meanwhile, the Darwin branch of the Australian Skeptics got into the act. Spokesman Simon Potter came up with the theory that the humble ceiling fan was responsible for the rock throwing. He invited the *Northern Territory News* to his house to demonstrate that all you need to do is place steak knives or gravel on top of the fan, turn the fan on and, *voilà*, instant poltergeist activity. Not surprisingly, the residents were fed up with 'knockers', so Simon was not welcome at the house. Besides, it is hardly likely that the mother of a baby would deliberately set up flying steak knives. Maybe Potter should have spoken to Brendon Gowdie, who used his thermal imaging camera to provide further substantial evidence. Gowdie, who normally used the camera for his building maintenance business, was hired especially for the job by 'Today Tonight'. His task was to examine objects immediately they were thrown, to determine whether there were heat-induced fingerprints.

Gowdie had difficulty because the ambient temperature was close to normal skin temperature, but he admitted the results were beyond his comprehension:

> There was definitely infra-red energy on the objects, but it was completely uniform—like a force field. If someone threw a steak knife, for example, they'd have to hold every part of its surface evenly for three or four seconds and then throw it while still holding it that way. As a technician, I went there looking for logical solutions, but nothing about the place added up. It'd be quite wrong to assume that the suspicion over Kirsty explains all this, because things were happening when she wasn't even there.

Other professional crews were equally perplexed. Danny Sim and assistant Jarrod Suttie, on assignment for Channel 7, also provided strong supporting evidence. Danny is a very experienced operator and has an open mind, especially after witnessing a remarkable incident during a two-and-a-half-year stint in Jakarta. He showed me the remarkable footage he took of a fireball soccer match, where the ball is wrapped in string and doused in diesel. As we watched, he described the action:

> After kicking the flaming ball around barefooted for a while they put on another extraordinary act. One of [the team] members, in a state of deep trance and wearing only a pair of pants, had gallons of sulphuric acid poured over his head. We were trying to film it but started to get affected by the acrid fumes and smoke. Heaps of people were there, holding their noses to avoid fumes. We had to move away to continue filming. Five minutes later, we returned to where he was standing and a hole was burnt in the asphalt. Finally, he washed himself and to all intents and purposes appeared to be perfectly OK. I know most people I've

spoken to believe I'm bullshitting—but I saw it and filmed it. So I have some sympathy for the occupants at Humpty Doo putting their case to deaf ears.

Both Danny and Jarrod saw objects in flight, but not the initial movement. Danny spoke about one incident when he saw gravel materialise from nowhere. He focused on the fact that, in spite of the driveway gravel being soaked from heavy rain, the materialised gravel was warm and dry. Danny admitted the goings-on sometimes 'put the shits up him', particularly when he saw a carving knife fly around and stick into a wall. Both men saw, and shot, glasses being smashed and live bullets and batteries being 'thrown'. Jarrod reported 'heaps of noises when there was no one around', including sounds of big rocks being thrown on the roof and gravel coming out of the ceiling. Danny's uncanniest experience occurred when he was filming through the manhole cover in the roof:

> My job was to catch anyone who was hiding and chucking rocks or gravel. Others in the team were holding a ladder for me when I heard this bloody piece of glass, or something similar, hit the roof just near my ear. Next moment, this piece of glass hit the floor next to their feet. It appears the glass went through the roof and the ceiling instantaneously. I was looking up at the ceiling, so I had an excellent view when I heard it hit the roof and the next moment I saw it in mid-air and land next to their feet. All I heard from the boys was, 'Oh shit!' It was really unbelievable!

Later Danny was filming on the shed, taking wide shots, when gravel fell on the roof of the car beneath where he was filming. If that wasn't enough an A4 battery appeared, bounced on the roof, and hit the cameraman with considerable force on the head. 'I was getting paranoid because there was writing on the walls saying, 'Media go' and 'Media die', he recalled.

> Next, a spanner thumped on the roof, creating this tremendous noise, and I nearly shat myself. And while I

was filming the spanner a rock landed beside me and I said to myself, 'That's enough' because it really put the wind up me.

There was one strange aspect of Danny's recollection of these events: the thump on the head with the battery created an aching head for more than an hour, yet there was no sign of a cut or a lump, and no sign of bruising.

Danny continued,

> Stavros Kanaris, the bloke who built the house, had to sell it because he was bankrupt and there's no two ways about it he was pissed-off about losing his home. He told me that during construction he'd sent his daughter out into the yard to get a stick to prop something up and when she returned she had this 'black fella's' spear. She told her father the Aboriginals claimed there were spirits on that land.

The Aboriginal connection did not stop there. Kirsty, at home alone, noticed two very black 'bush' Aborigines digging a hole next to the house. This was unusual, to say the least, because the property is surrounded by a cyclone fence and the house is more than 70 metres from the road. When Kirsty asked what they were doing they silently departed, leaving a cleared area about 1 by 2 metres around the 30-centimetre–deep hole. Was it an Aboriginal burial ground? No one could answer. In any case, their visit did have one benefit because, to the delight of the residents, the activity stopped for four days.

When he'd been out at the property doing some contract maintenance, Stavros Kanaris told Danny that he'd kept a diary hidden in the wall when he was building the house. 'It must still be there,' he said, 'because 10 years after the house was built I pulled the diary out and added to it.' 'While I was there,' Danny told me, 'Kanaris cut through the wall, but the friggin thing wasn't there. He couldn't believe it—I can tell you it was weird.

> That wasn't the end of it. Later I was talking to another tradesman, George. He was a painter who was hired to cover up words like 'You're going to die'. Well, he painted

over the numerous scribblings and took his tins of paint back to his car, when a bloody great heap of glass landed over his vehicle. George yelled out, 'That's enough for me ... I'm fuckin out of here!' Before he left, though, he reluctantly agreed to be interviewed. Kirsty was holding the baby in one hand and the mike in the other while I filmed. As I held the camera and George was spruiking, a bullet, glass and a shower of gravel flew past. And, when a another shower of glass hit his car, George had the shits up properly and just wanted out. He told me he was going home, having a few beers and taking the rest of the day off.

Danny questioned why Channel 7 didn't take a stronger approach because while the crew were sitting around the bar there would be knives and glass flying about.

'What was so intriguing was that the objects would hit and stop,' he recalled.. 'I remember a butcher's knife thumping on the table and stopping as though it was being blocked. If you threw it with the same force it would bounce and ricochet.' He insisted that if the residents were pulling a 'fast one' the crew would have caught them out. They set up heat sensors to detect people's movements, and seven cameras were strategically placed to ensure that all the residents were in sight 24 hours a day (apart from in their bedrooms). At one stage the crew secretly focused three cameras on the bar area, but they failed to catch any evidence of a hoax. Even a log was kept. Danny insisted that in 40 per cent of the cases it was impossible for the events to be created by the residents. 'It' was often in action when cameramen were facing the wrong way or 'it' would start again during battery changes on cameras, much to the frustration of the operators. Like so many other poltergeist cases 'it' appeared to be playing games with the protagonists. Both Danny and Jarrod agree that, in spite of the overwhelming evidence, they still have an open mind on the case. They also agree, though, that if it was a hoax it was a very expensive, very elaborate, very clever one.

The Darwin media and Sydney's Channel 7 beat the story up for all it was worth. Humpty Doo also hit the world's newsrooms.

Calls were received from American and European agencies. Even the BBC ran a story. The whole thing was at 'flash-point' when Channel 7 and *Northern Territory News* revealed on 23 April that Kirsty Agius had broken down and 'confessed' to reporter Greg Quail that she had thrown a plastic lid because the camera crew was not getting enough footage of ghostly happenings. All that was picked up by the cameras during four days and nights of filming was the motion of three objects—a baby's bottle inexplicably falling from the top of a microwave, a bullet in the final part of its trajectory, and the plastic lid 'flown' from behind a cupboard.

As is common with all poltergeist activity, the phenomenon is rarely seen in the first part of its movement and rarely captured on film. And because in this case so little evidence was filmed the 'plastic lid incident' became a big deal. Apparently Quail had grilled Kirsty late one night after viewing footage of a 'flying object'. The footage allegedly shows a reflection of Kirsty throwing the lid, which ricochets off a wall. The hoax story was spread through the Darwin when *Northern Territory News* reporter Nikki Voss wrote, 'She thought she was helping out, but Greg has told her she has blown it.' This 'admission', which was not recorded, was angrily denied by Kirsty. But 'Today Tonight' had its hoax story. Kirsty, still furious months later, told me Quail rang her up at midnight to question her about the footage. 'He continually harassed me on the phone until I replied in exasperation.

> I did it—is that what you want me to say? And then he replied, 'So you did.' He wasn't after the truth because he had already made up his mind. It was all crap: all that was picked up in the reflection was me shaking Jasmin's clothes before folding them up.

Danny said he didn't know whether Kirsty threw the object, but Jarrod Suttie was adamant:

> I can't see how she could have thrown the object because the angle and pace it was thrown made it nearly impossible. From the angle she's supposed to have thrown

the lid, it would have needed to change direction by 70 degrees in mid-air to strike the wall where it ended up. Even in the 'slow-mos' it shows just how fast the objects were travelling. In footage that went to air it all happened in two frames and there are 24 frames a second. Judging by where the object was frame by frame, I estimate it was moving around a metre in one twenty-fifth of a second. How could Kirsty throw something faster than test bowler Glen McGrath can bowl?

Shaking his head with frustration, Danny spoke his mind, 'If "Today Tonight" had shown the full story it would have been an absolute ball tearer!'

Soon after the 'revelation', and without confirming facts through Darwin ABC report Tracy Farrer, ABC's 'Media Watch' host Richard Ackland jumped on the bandwagon, suggesting that the tenants were tricksters who'd 'done it for the money'. This was nonsense. The tenants were quite open about the 'fortune' paid: $400 each. All of them agreed they would have given the money back to be rid of the entity and be allowed to stay in the house. 'Media Watch' often criticises others for their lack of diligence, so it is surprising the show's producer, at least, did not arrange for a researcher from the Darwin office of the ABC to check the facts. If they had checked with Farrer, for example, their story might have been very different. Farrer, a former science technician, said, 'I saw things flying in front of my face. Science is my background but I can't explain it in logical terms, but I know what I saw and it wasn't a hoax.'

Greg Quail earlier told the *Northern Territory News*, after his team of five had spent four days living at the McMinn's Lagoon house, that they were still sceptics:

> But all were convinced there was something going on inside and around the house ... We saw things flying around the house, including knives, and we can't work out how they were propelled. Our news team took seven cameras in the house, one of which recorded thermal

imagery. If someone had thrown knives and other objects it would have been recorded on the thermal camera, yet there was no evidence.

And four days before Kirsty's 'confession' Quail wrote a column for the *Sunday Territorian* of 19 April 1998 that indeed confirmed his belief that there was paranormal activity at Humpty Doo. He said his scepticism was immediately aroused when the story broke on April 1, but then

> For four days we endured an onslaught of flying scissors, stones, knives, broken glass and, yes, three live bullets. Not once did any of us see even a suggestion that any of the five residents of the alleged 'Haunted House of Humpty Doo' was trying to pull a swiftie. Neither did our seven cameras!

One wonders whether the Sydney management at Channel 7 had pre-judged the story or decided it was time to wrap it up because the ratings were slipping. And, indeed, while I was still working in Darwin a senior journalist at Channel 8 said he was still convinced the whole thing was a set-up by the residents.

Jill spoke of her frustration, saying all of them were infuriated when they were accused of lying or making money from 'it':

> You have to realise how we felt because the story was broadcast around Australia and appeared in any number of newspapers. Relatives and friends were ringing up and saying, 'What are you doing?' because, underneath, they all started to think we were idiots. Besides, our phone bill was outrageous during our attempts to find someone who could help us. I'm not religious—in fact, none of us are religious and none of us have mucked around with ouija boards or any type of black magic that might attract this sort of attention. Anyway, I felt privileged by the experience and it has made me believe there is something out there, something beyond our earthly existence—I'm not sceptical anymore!

Dave was more pragmatic: 'We were putting all the bits and pieces that had been thrown back into a drawer, in a cupboard outside the house, but the contents kept coming back again—it was as though the "fucking thing" was continually taking the piss out of us.'

I also felt during my experiences with Liz that the poltergeist was out to make fun of me. But that's unusual: many witnesses of poltergeist activity speak about the 'joker' element.

Kirsty also reflected on the attention 'it' created. She said some of the interstate visitors were OK but, apart from Jack Ellis, the Darwin media tried to make fools of them.

> When Channel 7 rang us from Sydney and said they would pay us to cover the story we agreed, saying they could have the story if they found someone to get rid of 'it' because we liked living in that house ... It was rumoured we got thousands of dollars but that was bullshit. They were supposed to stay for one afternoon and they stayed for four days and nights, with lights and cameras. When they were there all other media were excluded, which we didn't mind because we were sick of all the attention. In the end we were really upset, though, because they just made idiots of us, even though the 'Today Tonight' team all experienced phenomena.

Interestingly, in June 1999, during a week's secondment in Darwin, I spoke to Nikki Voss and asked about her perspective on the case now, a year or so later. At the time Nikki had been Chief of Staff at *Northern Territory News*. 'It's difficult for reporters not to take a cynical perspective on such cases—otherwise it would appear to our reading public that we are gullible,' she said.

> But I personally saw objects fall off tables during my visits and on one occasion witnessed a glass beer mug thrown with considerable force through a hole in one of the broken windows. The precision of the trajectory was amazing because only millimetres separated the sides of the mug from the hole in the glass. All I will say is that there was something not right there.

Meanwhile, Dave wondered about the owners, of the rented house who were living a couple of hundred metres away in a partitioned tin shed, with five children and in 40-degree summer heat: 'You have to ask why they chose to rent that place when they owned a perfectly reasonable house with a swimming pool and a great bar area.

> For a moment we even thought that the owner might want to move into the house, when he put an eviction notice on us at midnight. He said he wanted us out the next day because we'd trashed his house. When we appeared in court the judge really laughed at us and said, 'I don't believe in ghosts', and that was the end of it. I told the judge we were not trashing the house and that we didn't know what was causing the damage.

* * *

Darwin residents continued to follow the fascinating story through the *Northern Territory News*, which reported on 16 April 1998 'An eviction notice had been served on the tenants of the Humpty Doo house. The owners of the rented house, Kosta and Angela Boubaris, said they were shocked when they returned from their Queensland holiday to find "spirits" were allegedly responsible for trashing the house,' readers were informed.

> On 16 April 1998 Magistrate Greg Cavanagh heard an application for an eviction order by Mr and Mrs Boubaris. The couple requested the immediate eviction of the tenants because of damage done to the house. Mr Cavanagh warned the tenants it was a legal matter and advised them he did not believe in ghosts or the supernatural. He said if there was any damage in the house while they were occupying it then it might be sufficient to evict them.

Repairing the damage cost the five around $800. But, as they pointed out, apart from smashed windows and holed flyscreens, most of the damage was done to personal possessions—crockery, glasses, ornaments, wedding gifts, sentimental items that could never be replaced. One has to ask again why would they want these destroyed? Commonsense prevailed and the eviction notice was overturned when lawyers for the owners admitted that the house was generally in good condition. For the five, though, the eviction notice was the last straw and they all left in early May.

Kirsty, Andrew and baby Jasmin moved 100 kilometres away to Adelaide River. Jill and Dave moved to another rental property a few kilometres away. Murph spends most of his time fishing and lives in other digs. None of them has had experiences like that since.

Kirsty, totally exasperated with their detractors, pointed out,

> I was forever cleaning up fine glass from smashed light bulbs. Why would I want to do that when I had a small baby? I was there all the time when the others worked. Believe me, I would rather have worked. Yes, I've seen something few others have, but I didn't enjoy it!

Dave, in his laconic way, said, 'What really pissed me off was that the "fucking thing" was living there without paying rent!'

Frank Robson left Darwin wrestling with what he'd seen but convinced that reports of the whole thing being a hoax were ridiculous. 'I saw the looks on the faces of other impartial investigators when steak knives, live bullets and other sharp objects smashed into walls and tables,' he told me.

> Virtually every time it appeared unlikely for any of the people in the house at the time to have contrived the events. It's something entirely beyond my experience. It's absurd to think someone could be doing it manually!

As for me, I wondered about the Trident formed with stones in Murph's bedroom. Why was it formed? Was the Canberra poltergeist continuing to exploit me, knowing I would investigate the case, that I would 'lock-on' to the description of that beautifully formed medieval sign? Again bikes were involved: Murph's Kwaka, Dave's Harley, and of course the possible connection with my Triumph Trident?

Not long after my final chat with Dave and Jill, I had plenty of time to think about the 'tenuous association' during my flight from Darwin to Canberra in June 1999. Over my usual gin and tonic I tried to rationalise the possibility that the 'intelligence' was still playing games with me, this time using the Trident symbol to deepen the mystery that maybe all poltergeist activity is somehow connected to a common 'external agency'. If only I knew!

Seeking solutions: riding on the edge
10

Whenever I'm feeling jaded I seek rejuvenation through riding motorbikes—preferably powerful bikes. There's something about the freedom, and even the risk-taking associated with biking that concentrates and distils the mind. Maybe it's the rush of air, or the immediacy of the surrounds, or simply the adrenalin kick that comes with riding a 100 bhp machine. Although it all depends on my mood. If I'm in a contemplative frame of mind, a quiet potter through the countryside on a summer day, letting the warm air caress my face, gives me that feeling of being at one with myself and the world. On the other hand, if I feel frustrated or particularly exuberant I know it won't be long before I have to spend another $500 on a set of soft compound sports tyres.

In July 1995 Canberra was enduring a particularly cold winter. It was early on a Sunday morning and I felt stiff and uncomfortable from the previous day's golf. I am always amazed at how much more my body suffers when I've had a disastrous round. This became very apparent when I bent down to stoke up the wood burner: my back felt as unyielding as the shaft on my driver. I limped back across the room to my Mac computer, wondering as

I flicked it on whether the spirits would mess around with it, as they had with my bike. Could they remove or add information? They seemed to have little trouble manipulating the material recorded for Liz's 'love tapes'. While the Mac warmed up I drew the curtains aside, noting the thick layer of frost on the lawn. As usual, I made excuses to myself about starting to write. I switched on the radio and made myself a coffee to stop me from staring at a blank screen. The broadcaster on the 7.00 am news said the temperature outside was a chilly minus four.

I soon found myself pacing around the house like a caged tiger, wondering what I had let myself in for. I knew if the book was published I would cop a lot of flack and so would Liz. Many people would ridicule me, yet I knew I was telling the truth. It seemed as though someone, or something, had instilled in me an obsession with completing this work, in spite of the fact that I made more money on the stock exchange in a day than I did from my previous book. I couldn't help myself: I had to continue.

But there was so much material—so many unanswered questions—and it was leaving me with a deep frustration. Even interviewing Liz was very difficult. Although she is very intuitive and intelligent, she has a totally undisciplined mind and jumps from subject to subject with frightening speed as another spirit story or a more outrageous activity with a client comes to mind. Her mother had told me Liz was a beautiful pianist: I wondered where she had found the patience to learn. Liz always spoke with an earnest, impatient intensity and became annoyed if anyone questioned her recall. I was concerned further down the track that she would 'lose her cool' if interviewed by a probing, sceptical journalist or broadcaster. I, too, was having doubts and questioning my own observations.

I recalled my meeting with British parapsychologist Professor David Fontana in Rajasthan, India, in February 1994. We were both guests at the Brahma Kumaris World Spiritual University. Professor Fontana, an engaging person, has a deep interest in the paranormal and he impressed me with his understanding and knowledge. When I visited England the following year, on RAAF business, I discovered that he had been appointed President of the prestigious Society for Psychical Research. Most of our conversation back in India was about *Flight into the Ages*, my book on paranormal activity in the military.

Only later, when I read of his investigations into a fascinating poltergeist case in South Wales (see Chapter 11), did I learn that he too had doubts when he observed phenomena. Although he had ample evidence—from his own sightings and from reliable witnesses—he still questioned the evidence in the 'cold, hard light of day'. I was in a similar position. I had a considerable amount of evidence and I trusted my own judgment, but when I told friends what I was involved in most of them laughed and wanted to know whether I was smoking dope or if Caressa had me 'hooked'.

I especially remember regaling a number of senior officers at RAAF Richmond the evening before leaving to take part in Exercise Kangaroo 95 in northern Australia. They thought I was a bit loopy and yet, on questioning, they revealed that they too had had experiences they could not explain. A few red wines had been consumed, and the stories about Caressa and her clients struck the right chord, eliciting a string of hilarious yarns about the officers' own youthful 'experiments' with prostitutes in Thailand and Malaysia. They had not experienced conflict—these were their 'war stories', where no one really got hurt and, in those days, if you did 'get the clap' a few jabs from the medic fixed the problem. But other friends—and, strangely, a high proportion of military pilots and navigators—were intensely curious. What is it about air crew? It was the same with *Flight into the Ages*: it was the 'airframe operators' who showed the greatest interest and, indeed, had had the greatest number of unexplained experiences.

I walked outside with my coffee, the steamy haze from the cup reminding me how cold it was. Wandering around the yard, reminding myself that gardening wasn't my forte, I peered through the garage window at my Triumph, sitting forlornly on the centre stand. I hadn't started, let alone ridden, the bike for a couple of weeks. It had been too cold! While I gazed at the machine I wondered just how the spirits—unless, of course, some joker was having a giant lend of me—had managed to place the gold-covered rocks so precisely on the bike. One exactly in the middle of my seat and other exactly in the middle of the petrol cap. Or how 'they' had summoned the energy to 'throw' a stone and hit me in the middle of my back as I walked down Liz's driveway to put the bike under shelter, away from the rain. And how—and this one had me completely baffled—'they' had contrived to manipulate the throttle by turning the idle screw through half a dozen turns, which inevitably made the engine rev uncontrollably. That manoeuvre had me stumped!

Did Liz really have an accomplice lurking in the shadows just to fool me? Yes, it wouldn't have been hard for someone familiar with motorbikes to manipulate the idle screw. It also wouldn't have been difficult to place the rocks on the seat and petrol cap. Or for that matter to hit me in the back with the rock, although it was a pretty good shot—fair between the shoulder blades. But why?

First, Liz didn't know, although it was a reasonable assumption, that I was going to ride my bike that night. She told me later that she pleaded with her spirit friends to fix my bike, despite the fact that she'd asked them to 'empty the petrol tank' or 'let the air out of the tyres.' For an accomplice, letting the air out would have been relatively simple but emptying the tank would have been more difficult because the petrol cap was locked. Second, the accomplice would have needed to know that 'gold- covered rocks' were also manifesting in the house, to maintain 'phenomenon consistency'. And if they were going to maximise the effects surely they would have pushed the mirrors through more than just 30 degrees. I admit that because the bike was not under my constant surveillance it would not have been difficult to 'create' these things. On the other hand, Liz was well aware of my strict adherence to the truth. If I'd had any inkling the events were contrived, and if my doubts had been proven true, I would have dropped my investigation immediately. To the best of my knowledge nothing was falsified.

And finally—and this is important—when I reached my house and put the centre stand down accidentally there was no accomplice there to flick the side stand down. Yet that is exactly what happened. The side stand was already activated against the spring loading before I glanced down to make sure my foot was on the correct lever. So I was left with the crazy notion that I was dealing with an intelligent poltergeist that knew the basic workings of a motorbike. One theory about poltergeists is that the power is generated through the agent—Liz. Yet Liz had no idea of the workings of my motorbike, so I was left to conclude that there must be 'courses' on motorbike maintenance on the 'other side'. Ridiculous, I know, but I was running short of ideas. And what's so special about a motorbike? If a poltergeist can make a small object 'go through solid walls', why not dematerialise a large object such as the Triumph? I knew there had been instances of 'ghost bikes' appearing and disappearing. Were these cases of false perceptions, mind-altering drug, or 'real' vision?

In her book *Understanding Ghosts*, Canadian author Victoria Branden writes of an encounter with a 'phantom motorcyclist'. During a long and tiring drive, she realised she was wandering all over the road, driving unsafely. She decided to pull over, and as she did so she saw a man standing astride his parked motorbike, glaring at her with 'vicious hostility'. Thoughts of terror arose in her, but the motorcyclist vanished ... dematerialised. When she got out of her car with her dog, she and the dog were violently ill—apparently the result of a faulty starter-spray can. She, quite reasonably, put the apparition down to a 'fumes-oppressed brain'. But there have been other cases of phantom motorcyclists. What imprint, what emotion, what psychic process produces these images that are perceptible to the human eye, yet physically don't exist?

Late one very cold night in January 1967, this time in England, David Pike of Priory, Wellington, was returning home from Taunton on his motor bike. The 18-year-old builder's labourer was approaching a crossroads on the A38 trunk road leading to Poole when a 'phantom motorcyclist' came racing towards him from the other direction, closely followed by a Triumph car. The car's headlights outlined the rider, producing a 'halo' that embraced the cyclist's body. As the pair were about to cross, the motorcyclist suddenly swerved towards Pike, causing him to brake frantically. Just as the 'phantom' and Pike were about to collide, the motorbike and its rider vanished. Pike said he couldn't understand why he hadn't hit him: 'If there had been anything there, I know I would have done so.' The startled Pike stopped and examined the area but and found nothing—no tracks, no motorcyclist. The rider and his bike had simply vanished. On questioning, the driver of the Triumph said he had neither heard nor seen a motorcyclist, which did not help to console the shaken young motorcyclist.

Even the legendary T.E. Lawrence, better known as 'Lawrence of Arabia', is the subject of an unsolved motorcycle mystery. Following his heroic feats in World War 1, leading an Arab revolt against their Turkish overlords, Lawrence had escaped the public's gaze by joining the Royal Air Force. The former colonel who was awarded the Companion of the Order of the Bath, the Companion of the Distinguished Service Order and the Croix de Guerre led an extraordinary dual existence as an aircraftsman in the RAF while at the same time maintaining close friendships with notables such as George Bernard Shaw, Winston Churchill and Lady Astor. In 1923 he rented a cottage called 'Clouds Hill' and from this haven wrote his epic, *The Seven Pillars of Wisdom*. But, although he regarded 'Clouds Hill' as an 'earthly paradise', he still missed the excitement of his previous exploits. Some compensation was provided by high-speed rides on his powerful Brough Superior bikes. Lawrence developed a great affinity with Broughs and always owned the latest model—he bought seven of the bikes between 1922 and 1935. The thundering V twin was one of the most powerful bikes of the day and could exceed the 'ton' with relative ease, if not comfort. Lawrence described in his book *The Mint* racing a Bristol Fighter at speeds of over 100 mph without goggles or crash helmet. No wonder many of his friends disliked the noisy, thunderous bikes he rode and prophetically warned Lawrence of the dangers of reckless, high-speed driving along narrow country lanes.

In May 1935, when Lawrence was riding from the Bovington RAF Camp to his beloved 'Clouds Hill', he was killed avoiding a boy cyclist. And it would seem that part of Lawrence has never left the area. Apart from reported sightings of his ghostly form in Arab dress, several people claim to have heard the throaty roar of the Brough coming towards them, usually at about dawn. But as they listened, waiting for the bike to appear, the noise would abruptly stop. The witnesses either were people who had heard Lawrence's bike when he was alive or were motorcycle enthusiasts, who could easily recognise the distinct beat of the large twin. Was it Lawrence's machine, the noise somehow locked in time? Who knows.

There is something special about motorbikes. Like so many motorcycle enthusiasts, Lawrence became 'addicted to' that euphoria, a oneness with the machine and a closeness to nature that occasionally transforms the ride into a spiritual experience. For a split second, even a former 500 cc world champion experienced an 'out-of-body' sensation, similar to that experienced by fighter pilots who see themselves outside the cockpit; Air Force doctors call this 'break-off' phenomenon. And it was motorcycles that inspired Robert Pirsig in the mid-1970s to wax philosophical in his classic, *Zen and the Art of Motorcycle Maintenance*. One *New York Times* reviewer wrote of the book, 'Profoundly important ... full of insights into our most perplexing contemporary dilemmas ... intellectual entertainment of the highest order'. In essence, Pirsig used the motorcycle as a 'mobile backdrop' to explain complex philosophical questions. It was a book I read avidly towards the end of my university studies because of my interest in philosophy and, of course, motorbikes.

Trying to put some logic into my investigations surrounding Liz, I re-read Pirsig's book and came across a conversation he'd had with some friends while riding across America:

> I don't get upset when scientists say that ghosts only exist in the mind. It's that 'only' that gets me. Science is only in your mind too, but that doesn't make it bad. Or ghosts either. Laws of nature are human inventions, like ghosts.

Laws of logic, of mathematics are also human inventions, like ghosts. The whole blessed thing is a human invention, including the idea that it isn't a human invention. The world has no existence whatsoever outside the human imagination. It's all a ghost, and in antiquity was so recognised as a ghost, the whole blessed world we live in is run by ghosts. We see what we want to see because these ghosts show it to us, ghosts of Moses and Christ and the Budda, and Plato, and Descartes and Rousseau and Jefferson and Lincoln, and on and on. Isaac Newton is a very good ghost. One of the best. Your common sense is nothing more than the voices of thousands and thousands of these ghosts from the past. Ghosts trying to find their way among the living.

Well, which ghost, which memory, was seeking to place a message through Liz and me? I really didn't know but, in spite of Pirsig's musings, which I felt only encouraged inaction, I believed my only option was to concentrate on research, to see if there were parallel cases. Then—ghostly imaginings or not—I would be able to confirm or reject my own observations. I read every book I could find on the subject. I wrote to Professor Fontana and to Professor Bob Morris, who heads Edinburgh University's Parapsychology Department, to ask if they had any knowledge of a similar case and whether intense sexual activity produces poltergeist activity. Unfortunately I didn't get the answers I was after. I was rapidly coming to the conclusion, though, that poltergeists, far from simply demonstrating random 'mischievousness', on occasions exhibit intelligence. Quite apart from what had happened to my Triumph, how else could I explain the appearance of small flashlight moments after I had asked Liz for a torch and she'd told me there wasn't one in the house? What powers could I attribute to Liz and her 'friends'? My study of poltergeist activity had not brought to light a story of anyone being murdered, although when I was researching in the RAAF museum at Point Cook, near Melbourne, some years earlier I came upon the tale of a fireman who felt as though he was being strangled by an unseen force and refused to work his night shift. Liz and Donna experienced being 'slapped', which resulted in 'physical' red marks.

Ultimately, what impressed me in these cases—because you tend to question your own powers of observation—was the evidence provided by the nine other witnesses in Liz's case. Certainly, a number of them queried, as have I, whether what they experienced was 'real'. I believe one, two, or even three, people could be fooled, but it's difficult to fool nine from such diverse backgrounds. The sheer weight of evidence made it difficult to dismiss the phenomena or attempt to explain them by logical means.

During my visit to England in mid-1995—to facilitate research for an ABC documentary on the history of the Australian Flying Corps and the RAAF—I followed up my correspondence, phoning Professor Morris at Edinburgh University to ask for his advice on reference material relating to poltergeists. He suggested a book by noted parapsychologist Dr Alan Gauld. I managed to contact Dr Gauld at his home in Nottingham and he said that although his book was out of print there were a couple of bookshops outside London where second-hand copies were available. It appears, however, that the spirits were also helping: I found a second-hand copy at Skoob Books, within walking distance of my hotel. The shop had bought the book a couple of days before my inquiry.

In his book, written with A.D. Cornell, Gauld notes that in 79 of 500 cases surveyed 'communication' took place. In other words, the 'entity' was in one way or another responsive to questions, requests, and the like, and perhaps 'answered back'. Gauld goes onto to say, 'For present purposes it will suffice if we agree that there are some poltergeist cases, and some hauntings too, in which the phenomena sometimes appear as if controlled by an intelligent agency.' In the final chapter, though, the authors conclude,

> We do not think that much further progress is likely with regard to these problems, or any other very numerous problems that arise in connection with poltergeist phenomena, until sustained and competent investigations

have been conducted into the nature and point of origin of the physical force.

So what is this force? If highly qualified and experienced researchers have failed to explain it then I have little chance: all I can do is observe as possible.

As I said earlier, Liz had specifically asked her spirit friends to impress me by doing something to my bike. Anyone who knows me reasonably well could predict my reaction to someone or something messing with my bike. Liz was delighted that her 'friends' had jammed the throttle; I, on the other hand, had a complete 'sense of humour failure'. Friends of Liz's know that she has trouble keeping a secret. If she'd had an accomplice surely she would have had difficulty controlling her exuberance whilst playing at being amazed. Regardless, whether it was Liz's accomplice or the poltergeist, they chose wisely, knowing I have an affinity with bikes that is stronger than anything I've felt for machines with four wheels. If it were an 'intelligent' poltergeist that night it was as though 'it' was out to play a game with me, to impress me of a dimension I was seeking to probe. I was being teased and seduced by a spirit tempter who refused to remove her ghostly veil. Not once was 'its' action malevolent and, when I thought I had seen enough, back it came with manifestations that were even more sensational. At the end of the evening when Liz insisted that there was going to be one more dramatic action—sure enough, that's what happened.

Philosophers have tried, and priests have tried, to explain what is on the 'other side': do we really become invisible yet in touch with earthly surrounds? No one has produced a totally satisfactory answer. Maybe poltergeist activity is but a piece in the complex jigsaw. Maybe we will learn more as we fit the pieces together. But why would we want to 'hang around' earthbound when most religions suggest that 'life' beyond is far more interesting than our own. Liz is convinced of life on the 'other side' and has never wavered from her intention of committing suicide when her body starts to deteriorate. She wants to be recognised—she wants fame, however transient. She feels no discomfort about wanting to move from the material world to the spiritual when the time is right. So is she responsible for unleashing this force? Or is she just a puppet of something no one fully understands? How can she talk to 'Matt' on the phone? Maybe she is having a 'lend of me', but I doubt it. She is too obsessed by her 'friends'.

Does she always tell the truth? Liz is often brutally candid, but how can a prostitute always tell the truth? As she constantly emphasises, prostitution is about illusions, about making men, and women, feel good about themselves. Is she going to tell an ugly man he's ugly, an impotent man that he should get an erection, or an insecure man that he's a loser, or chastise a married man for infidelity? Of course not. Liz is paid not only for giving physical satisfaction but also to boost her clients' self-esteem, however temporarily. So does her sexual activity attract the spirits? I really didn't know.

There were too many questions, too many intangibles, and not enough answers. No wonder I was having trouble finishing the story: the frustration was eating at me. I turned on the small electric heater beside my desk to full blast, to supplement the inadequate wood fire, and sat staring at my computer. I seemed to be brain-dead. Nothing. I looked outside and watched the watery sun trying to break through: it was having no effect on the thick frost. I sat back in my chair, hands behind my head and gazed hypnotically at the white carpet outside my widow. Finally, I snapped out of this fixation with the frost. 'Bugger it,' I growled to myself. 'I need some fresh air.'

I pushed back my seat, walked over to the cupboard and pulled on my thick waterproof trousers and the fox-racing jumper with the thermal lining, laced up my boots, zipped up my jacket, and thumped out to the garage. I pulled up the roller door, heaved the bike off the centre stand, and yanked it outside. Triumphs don't leak oil any more but they're still bloody hard to start on freezing mornings. (This has now been fixed by the installation of a new black box.) I finally fired up the big triple and slid on my silk balaclava, helmet and thick winter gloves. My neighbour, who was looking out her window, shook her head as I idled down the driveway. The cold numbed my face when at the lights I lifted my helmet visor to prevent fogging.

The chill soon crept through my thick protective gear, but it couldn't anaesthetise my frustration. There was no traffic on the road: sensible people were still in bed. I drove to the Cotter turn-off, through the traffic lights, past the former Joint Services Staff College at Weston, and then towards Uriarra Crossing—a favourite with motorcyclists and speed cops in good weather. I knew it was unlikely that anyone, let alone patrolling police would be on the roads on this damp and freezing morning. It wasn't long before that seething frustration turned to the throttle hand.

I love motorbikes! I've owned 10 of them since gaining my licence at the age of 17. The last was a Suzuki VX800, which I sold with little more than 4000 kilometres on the clock to buy the Triumph simply because the VX had all the attributes on paper and on paper only. A bike has to feel right; it has to have soul. Even the exhaust note on the VX sounded like an emaciated fart. I have ridden many bikes—including Honda's Super Blackbird, the superb Kawasaki ZX-9, and even a 250 kph blast on the brutally quick ZX-12—but the British racing green and cream Triumph is the most evocative bike I have owned. Maybe it's the spine tingling note from the triple at 9000 rpm plus, the simple roadster construction, or is it reliving memories of my youthful exuberance flaunting death at the controls of my first Triumph. Regardless I probably treat it much better than any girlfriend. It is always there, like a faithful dog, and it responds superbly in spite of my constant abuse. Today I knew it was going to be abused.

When the road allowed, I screwed the throttle round to the stops in second gear and the bike just squatted down at the rear and took off like a rocket sled. As I hit the 9500 rev limit the speedo was reading 120 kph, well over the speed limit. I flicked the gear lever into third without using the clutch and continued the surge, my arms being pulled from the grips by the rush of air and the sheer acceleration. For some reason the rev counter seemed to defy the ignition cut-out and spun past 10,000 rpm—160 kph, the old magic ton. I held it there for a moment, the engine screaming, the air ripping at my throat like an icy scalpel, before kicking the lever into fourth. In spite of all my protective clothing that awful chill beckoned me to destruction, as though I was being called by the mystical sirens. I was a fighter pilot suffering target fixation and I had to make a conscious effort to detach myself from the effects of the adrenalin coursing through my veins.

Into fifth, and now the tortured machinery had become an extension of my mind, the blurred scenery an escape from reality. Time ceased to exist, my brain fixated totally on this mad, two-wheeled gallop across the deserted, ghostly countryside. Brake hard, drop down two gears, counter steer, cut the apex through the bend, foot pegs nearly scraping, throttle to the stops again, and so it went on—the hands, feet and body working in practised harmony, the Triumph dutifully responding to my stupidity. I kept this up for about 10 minutes or so before self-preservation thankfully prevailed. I knew I was riding too fast, much too fast.

My adrenalin spent, I gently slipped back through the six-speed box and stopped. I switched off the ignition and just sat there motionless. My hands and feet appeared only as a physical manifestation—I was bloody frozen and could hardly move. What if a kangaroo or some other animal had crossed my path, or that small footprint on the tyres had hit an ice patch? Would I become the next spirit? Would I be able to influence objects or people? What games could I play? Yet I had just involved myself in a dangerous, heady, crazy game that was about as sensible as Russian roulette. I wasn't a racer and I knew it. I was so cold I had difficulty pulling the bike onto the centre stand before slowly wandering alongside the road. I don't think I could have walked any faster—not only because of my heavy clothing but also because of my chilled bones.

I looked around. The grass was still covered in heavy frost and a thin, cold mist hung there with the menace of an undertaker. Immediately to my left was an gnarled old gum tree bereft of leaves and to the right, across a small dam, was a farmhouse set comfortably at the base of a gently sloping, snow-topped hill. Its green roof was at odds with the surrounding trees bare of their summer foliage. Smoke was rising vertically from its brick chimney, the only movement in this frosty, ghostly, surreal panorama. I stared at the grey plume: it signified life. With the cold seeping deeper into my bones, I continued staring. My thoughts were of warmth, then family, children playing, mother making breakfast. I'd almost forgotten such simple pleasures. I had chosen the single path. Pulling off my helmet, I immediately became aware of the silence. Absolute silence—no birds, no animals, no traffic—nothing.

It reminded me of my year in Canada as a 21-year-old, when I climbed the Rockies with two friends. They were fitter and had gone on ahead while I dawdled some way behind them ... until I saw bear tracks. I stopped, transfixed, charged with a sense of foreboding. I could see no movement, but I had recently read about a couple of tourists who were killed by brown bears. On reflection, I didn't know whether I was scared or just curious, or both. But I do know I became increasingly uncomfortable, for there was absolute silence. I had never experienced it before and I found it frightening—no aural input, as though part of you had died. And once again the same experience. I seemed to have learnt nothing. What was I scared of: life, experience, death? Who knows? What I had done was bloody crazy. I had taken similar risks in my youth on old worn-out British twins, riding them way beyond my limited ability. But at least the speed in those days was controllable—my first bike, a Triumph 500 cc Speed Twin, would have been pushing it to reach 80 mph. But this modern Triumph could exceed the magic ton with three gears to go! I finally sat down on the grass verge, humming to myself to blot out the overwhelming silence, the feeling exacerbated by the onslaught against the senses of the previous 10 minutes.

In other circumstances what was before me would have been a setting of serenity, a time to sit and reflect, 'perchance to dream'. If I had driven out there in a heated car with my former girlfriend maybe it would have been different—or would it? Why did I feel this detachment, as though I was a mere visitor to this realm. Did I need the ride to remind me of my earthly responsibilities, instead of continually delving into the esoteric.

How could I criticise Liz for her desire to commit suicide when she felt her body could no longer attract men? She had spent a fortune on plastic surgery in her search for beauty and her continuing need for men to find her attractive. She is terrified of growing old. Yet she is not scared of death: death to her is a release, a time to commune with her spirit friends. And here I was, a 50-year-old taunting death, behaving like an irresponsible youth trying to impress a girlfriend from the high diving board. I was not as sure as Liz. In spite of my research into a past life as a Luftwaffe pilot, which gave me amazing evidence, the sceptical streak still runs through me. I had seen enough to know there is something special, something beyond our knowing consciousness, a universal jigsaw puzzle we do not understand. My research in the Philippines, watching and undergoing psychic surgery, was further proof.

As I sat dwelling on all this it slowly dawned on me that I was becoming far more interested in a hot shower and a steaming bowl of porridge when I got home than these philosophical issues. I knew if I'd continued riding like that I would need more than psychic surgery. I had work to do and I wasn't going to complete it thrashing aimlessly around the countryside. I got up and walked slowly back to the bike, turning around to stare at the rising plume of smoke, wishing I had an invitation to the farmhouse for breakfast. At that moment I wanted normality, conversation, the innocence of children—I felt very alone and detached.

I jabbed the starter button, the triple roaring immediately into life, pulled in the clutch, thumped the lever into first gear and gently rode away. My last thoughts before numbness overcame my body, and my mind, 'Why had I taken this path in life? Why had I met Liz? There was so much I needed to know. Mediums, psychics, religion, friends, lovers—few had provided answers, only more questions.

Supporting evidence
11

When I look back over my years of research, I see numerous incidents that defy logic. One I recall was 'table tilting', which occurred a few years ago during a week's course at Arthur Findlay College (run by the Spiritualist Church), at Stansted in the south of England. About fifty of us formed a circle while, if I recall correctly, four people from the group placed their hands on an antique table in the middle of the room. As we sang—to produce 'energy'—the table began to rock and develop a life of its own. The four lightly touched its top, to maintain its 'balance' as it moved around the room. Finally, it stopped in front of one of the assembled circle. The person 'chosen' was then given a 'reading' by a medium present. As we, the group, became more enthusiastic and animated the table responded with more violent movements towards the next 'customer'.

At the time I was convinced the four 'guides' were not initiating the movement: on the contrary, they seemed only just capable of keeping the hapless table under control. In fact, it was very funny watching the four—middle-aged as they were—trying to keep pace with the 'energised' table. Unfortunately, though, while we were all laughing during a particularly lively spell one of the table's legs collapsed and the session ended. The following day I spoke to more than 10 people about the incident and all were convinced that the table's movements were not contrived. Among those I spoke to was a former army officer, a veteran of World War II, and even he was mystified about the 'energised' table and could only conclude that the inanimate wooden structure was being 'powered' by some type of psychic force.

At the College I also witnessed transfiguration medium Jean Skinner at work. She is able to 'transfigure' the face of deceased relatives or friends to the recipient of her 'reading.' The 'mask' is formed through ectoplasm, which emanates from her eyes. I was so impressed with Jean's gifts I drove to Newcastle to interview her. Later, I was privileged to act as her assistant during demonstrations.

Another odd incident occurred in July 1995, when I was in England working on the ABC documentary on the Australian Flying Corps and the RAAF. The ABC crew and I stayed at one of England's most delightful country hotels, 'Petwood', in the heart of Lincolnshire. 'Petwood' has had an interesting history and during World War II it was used as an officers mess by the famous 617 (Dambuster) Squadron. While the crew filmed I walked around the tranquil gardens wondering just what memories were trapped in time by the emotions created by the awful losses suffered by 617 Squadron. As we were checking out an hour or so later, I asked the receptionist if there were ever any unusual happenings in the hotel. 'Oh yes,' she replied,

> It is not unusual for guests to ring or come down to reception in the early hours of the morning, bleary-eyed and sleepless, complaining about the noisy party in the bar downstairs. Of course, when they are shown the bar where so many famous RAF and RAAF personalities drank and held wild parties there is no sign of anyone.

I checked the bar before we left: only the pictures gazed innocently at me.

And I wondered whether we humans are the only species capable of being 'touched' by these mysterious forces. In his account of his epic Antarctic adventure in 1915, Sir Ernest Shackleton suggests penguins may be gifted with foresight. He described in great detail the end of his specially strengthened ship, *Endurance*. The 350-tonne barquentine bravely resisted the crushing ice for nine months before finally slipping beneath the ice. When the pressure on the ship's hull was at its climax eight emperor penguins suddenly appeared from a crack 100 metres away. He recalls that the penguins walking a little way towards the group, halted, and after a few ordinary calls proceeded to utter weird cries that sounded like a dirge for the ship. 'None of us had ever heard the emperors utter any other than the most simple calls or cries, and the effect of this concerted effort was almost startling,' he noted. A strange observation: Shackleton was a dour, fearless explorer.

It is worth pausing here to examine interpretations of the word 'poltergeist'. According to Lewis Spence, editor of the *Encyclopedia of the Occult*, 'poltergeist' is a German word for 'noisy spirit' (or rattling ghost), although Germans now prefer the word *Spuk*. Other countries use different names—the Maltese *hares*, the Russians *domovoy* and the Africans *tokolisi*. Whatever they are called, poltergeists are associated with a range of inexplicable physical occurrences. Spence says, 'Manifestations are at best puerile, purposeless tricks and, not infrequently, display an openly mischievous and destructive tendency.'

Many investigators these days prefer to use a more scientific term, RSPK (recurrent spontaneous psychokinesis), which they consider more accurately describes poltergeist activity. In essence, it means an ability to influence other people, objects or events without any known physical force. It can last from a few weeks to many years. Its literal meaning is 'psyche', meaning soul or mind, and 'kinesis' meaning movement or motion. In other words, movement by the mind. Uri Geller is one of the most famous exponents of psychokinesis, with his apparent ability to bend and break metal without exerting physical force. And Russian psychic Nina Kulagina has been filmed moving small objects such as pens, eggs and matches under a glass or plastic screen, to avoid hidden wires or influence through forced air. Although both psychics have undergone numerous scientific tests, there are still sceptics who refuse to accept that this is no more than conjuring.

I was particularly interested in finding *Poltergeist*, parapsychologist Harry Price's book. It 'just happened' that, whilst browsing through bookshops in London with my close German friend Sofie Reich, I picked up a copy of the book for a couple of dollars. (It was ironic that I was in Sofie's company because she had given me invaluable assistance with my book on paranormal activities in the military.) Price's view differs from that of Spence in that he differentiates between a 'polt' and a ghost:

> A poltergeist is an alleged ghost, elemental entity, agency, secondary personality, 'intelligence', 'power', spirit, imp, or 'familiar', with certain unpleasant characteristics. Whereas the ordinary ghost of our story-books is a quiet, inoffensive, timid, noiseless and rather benevolent spirit, usually with friendly feelings towards the incarnate occupants of any place where it has an abode, the poltergeist is just the reverse. According to the many reports of its activities, in all lands and in all ages, the poltergeist is mischievous, destructive, noisy, cruel, erratic, thievish, demonstrative, purposeless, cunning, unhelpful, malicious, audacious, teasing, ill-disposed, spiteful, ruthless, resourceful, and vampire. A ghost haunts; a poltergeist infests. A ghost prefers solitude; a poltergeist prefers company. A ghost seeks the half-light; a poltergeist will 'perform' in sunlight.

Although Price's adjectives are colourful, his comments are worth noting because he was one of the world's leading parapsychologists for more than 30 years starting in the 1920s. He was an assiduous researcher and was responsible for the exposure of a number of fake mediums and clairvoyants. I was particularly interested to find any cases where sexual energy induced poltergeist activity. Price was also interested in this association and investigated one very amusing case.

On a visit to Vienna Price attempted to obtain a sitting with a gifted medium named only as Frieda W. Although he failed to secure a meeting, he did end up chatting with Herr W, who told Price that during the early months of their marriage his wife's mediumship was strongly affected by their relationship. At the height of his and Frieda's sexual excitement, ornaments would sometimes fall off the mantelpiece in their bedroom or the alarm would start ringing. On one occasion all the pots and pans in the kitchen began dancing. An earth-shattering 'orgasm'!

I remember discussing Frieda's experience with a highly intelligent, liberal-minded woman in her late twenties who, in my opinion, had mediumistic abilities. With her face turning a pale shade of pink, she told me of an unusual experience during 'explosive phone sex' with her partner via a cordless phone. She said that as she approached orgasm she and her partner heard the rapid build-up of a strong, high-pitched tone. Her partner failed to hear any of her ultimate enjoyment and the noise dissipated with the ebb of her orgasm. She and her partner both wondered whether a strong burst of energy had been transmitted to create the interference. Taking that line of thought further, maybe Frieda's orgasm, and the presence of her husband, induced a quantum leap in psychic energy. I asked Liz if she'd had similar experiences but she replied, 'Unfortunately no.'

On a more mundane level, Liz, for example, occasionally played noughts and crosses with her spirits, using lipstick. She would place the figure in the appropriate area but had to walk out of sight before the next 'move' was made. Only once did she 'catch' her playing partner and even then 'something' threw the lipstick across the room, apparently in 'shock.' It might not be as thrilling as objects flying across the bedroom at the height of ecstasy, or as 'stimulating' as noughts and crosses, but poltergeist activity has been reported as the cause of various kinds of damage: spontaneous fires, water unaccountably appearing, mocking laughter, groans and screams, stones or objects being thrown, people being touched or smeared. Poltergeists are usually wary of investigators, which makes it extremely difficult to research them in a scientific way. More often than not, phenomena cease as researchers walk through the door and start again as they leave. Accusations of fraud are thus not uncommon, and sometimes true, but this does not help a family suffering from the antics of a genuine poltergeist. Unlike Liz, not all people feel comfortable with a poltergeist's attentions. And some people have used poltergeist activity for their own purposes; for example, in the United Kingdom there have been examples of families living in council houses who have used the 'ghost or poltergeist' trick to obtain better accommodation.

Poltergeist activity is recorded as far back as 856 BC. One early author noted that, regardless of whether the haunting is in 'civilised' or 'savage' countries, the phenomenon is invariably the same. Dr Alan Gauld says one of the earliest 'plausible' cases was recorded by Flavius Josephus in his *Antiquities of the Jews*, written about AD 94. Josephus witnessed a Jew named Eleazar, a noted exorcist of demons, causing a bowl of water placed remote from observers to be upset in front of Emperor Vespasian. Dr Gauld continues

> According to the theory advanced by spiritualists, this centre of the disturbances is a natural medium, through whom the spirits desire to communicate with the world of living beings. In earlier times such a person was regarded as a witch, or the victim of a witch, whichever supposition was best fitted to the circumstances.

Another theory suggests that poltergeist activity occurs in households where an individual is in an emotionally disturbed state, one that he or she is unable to understand. This produces repressed anger or fear, which generates the excess energy is required for the activity. It is frequently noted that poltergeists tend to centre around particular people, often adolescents and often girls. These people are usually referred to as poltergeist 'agents' or poltergeist 'mediums'. Invariably there are exceptions—Liz, who is 40, is one. So it's important to consider an academic opinion, in this case that of a psychiatrist, especially since Liz came under a 'shrink's care' during her late teens and early twenties. In 1972 psychiatrist Caroll Nash wrote the following in *Parapsychology Review*:

> Hysterical disassociation of an infantile part of the psyche in which severe conflicts are kept repressed may be the explanation for poltergeist phenomena. According to the American psychoanalyst Foder, a torn-off part of the mind that is conditioned by conflict material which the main personality has repressed uses psycho-kinesis to produce the paranormal psychic phenomena. Successful psychoanalysis would cure the underlying pathology, and remove the cause of the poltergeist.

Whether this is a reasonable theory I am unable to say. What I can say, though, is that the subject of my book underwent extensive psychoanalysis. But was it successful? Liz thinks not. As you see, the incidents concerning Liz are consistent with many other examples. But I believe it is the combination of incidents, the intensity of the phenomena and, most of all, the 'intelligence' behind the incidents that make the Liz Fleming case so fascinating. The question is, how can we measure the force of, or indeed hypothesise about, the 'mysterious creative mechanism' behind the case?

Before I discuss the experiences of others, it is worth noting the work of Emil Tizane, who researched hundreds of cases of RSPK investigated by French police from 1920 to 1950. He came up with nine consistent patterns associated with RSPK (as translated and condensed by Hans Bender).

1. Bombardment—often a house becomes the object of a hail of projectiles. Stones fall on the roof, break window panes, and penetrate through openings.
2. Bangs against the doors, the walls, or the furniture are heard.
3. Doors, windows, and even securely closed cupboards open themselves.

4. Objects are skilfully dislocated and thrown. Fragile ones often remain unbroken, even after a jump of a metre or more, while solid ones are sometimes completely destroyed.

5. Bizarre cracks and noises are sometimes noted.

6. Displaced objects do not show a regular trajectory: they behave as if they had been transported and even follow the contours of furniture.

7. In some rare instances, foreign objects penetrate into closed space.

8. When handled by observers, the objects feel warm.

9. Objects seem to form themselves in the air.

A case in Canada more than 100 years ago is pertinent. Esther Cox was an 18-year-old girl living in impoverished circumstances with her sister Jane in Amherst, Quebec. When Jane's boyfriend attempted to rape Esther poltergeist activity followed. The family had to cope with boxes being levitated and flung around the girl's bedroom and bedclothes being thrown from the bed—both to the accompaniment of loud, banging noises. Esther became more and more distraught and a doctor was called. He, too, became alarmed when he witnessed writing appearing on the wall; as he was leaving plaster broke off from part of the wall and travelled 'around the corner' to land at his feet. The doctor also reported sounds that were so loud they seemed like a sledgehammer pounding the shingle roof.

Esther started going into trances, which resulted in a minister being called. He was confronted by the sight of water being agitated in a bucket and appearing to boil in his presence. A visiting magician, Walter Hubbell, came to the house on a number of occasions and documented chairs falling over when he entered the room, plus being 'assaulted' with knives and other objects. Hubbell wrote a best-selling book about the case. His testimonies are said to be not totally reliable, but evidence from the family, a minister and a doctor is hard to ignore.

In African folklore there is a type of poltergeist, or *tokolisi*, reputed to have the power to drive people insane. One case involved a young girl of Hottentot descent, who was living on a farm in South Africa's Cape Province. Mary was eating a meal with her parents and was reaching out to take a potato from a bowl when a large clod of earth appeared from nowhere and hit the table beside her. Her startled family had no idea where the piece of earth had come from. But that was only the start. When the girl lifted a cup to her lips it was forced out of her hand and smashed on the floor. When she jumped up in alarm an unseen force sent her chair flying and gave her a vicious shove. In the ensuing days Mary was subjected to other, similar phenomena causing her to suffer. Finally, she was in such a state of terror she would wake at night, screaming. The distraught family was desperate and took the unusual step of seeking assistance of an African witchdoctor, who exorcised the malevolent force.

In 1904 at a Welsh farmhouse in Coedkernew, Gwent, poltergeist activity attracted the attention of the local constabulary. Bundles of hay were thrown into the yard, pictures were turned around on the walls, beds were moved, pickled cabbage was mixed with cream, 200 pieces of crockery were dropped in the kitchen without being broken, and the name of the woman's first husband was traced on the sooty glass of a lamp. In an attempt to ascertain the cause, ten people, among them the village policeman, sat up all night. Several hours passed with no activity, then a pat of butter flew across the room and hit the policeman in the eye. Maybe the 'boys in blue' these days would take their riot shields for protection against the unseen!

One of the most famous cases of poltergeist activity involves the English clergy. Borley Rectory was built in 1863 by the Reverend Henry Bull and housed a succession of priests and their families before it was gutted by fire in 1939. Literally hundreds of people, from scientists to investigating journalists from the BBC to RAF pilots have witnessed phenomena at the rectory, among them materialisations of objects; apparitions; women's voices; whisperings; sounds of galloping horses; scratchings; incessant bell-ringing; footsteps; knocks; thumps; wailing sounds; wall writings, often with pathetic messages; spontaneous locking and unlocking of doors; spontaneous falling of keys from locks; several outbreaks of fire; the disappearance and reappearance of objects; and 'matter-through-matter' events. A friend of Reverend Harry Bull (the son of Henry), Mr P. Shaw Jeffrey, a former headmaster, wrote to Harry Price from South Africa in 1942 about his experience. He said he and Bull had been friends at Oxford University and sometimes stayed together at the Rectory during the holidays.

> I had lots of small adventures at the Rectory. Stones falling about, my boots found on top of the wardrobe etc.; and I saw the 'nun' several times, and often heard the 'coach' go clattering by. But the big adventure that would have been worth your recording was one time when I missed a big French dictionary which I had been regularly using for some days. Nobody could find it, but one night I was awakened by a big bump on the floor and after I had lit my candle, there was the dictionary, with its back a good deal knocked about, sprawling on the floor. My bedroom door was locked.

He also wrote about another incident while he was visiting, with Harry, the neighbouring rectory, where Harry's brother Felix lived. Harry had said, 'Well Mary, cook says you can show us a few tricks—what about it?'

> The maid said nothing, but a tooth-glass came flying across from the wash stand behind the maids' back and circled gracefully around, hitting the jamb of the door just above my head. Just afterwards, the fender and fire irons and grate moved right across the room with a clatter. We bolted!

Another case I investigated concerned Bill and Dot Steele, who lived in the Canberra suburb of Higgins. The house was home to a friendly ghost, or poltergeist, from 1978 until 1988. 'He'—the Steeles gave it the male gender—'enjoyed' hot showers. During the ten years of 'his' residence, and always at night, Bill and Dot were woken more than a hundred times to the sound of a shower running. Invariably, when they went to investigate, the taps had been turned off but the shower recess was full of steam. The first time it happened, the couple thought one of their five children was playing a trick, but all were asleep.

Bill and Dot are not superstitious. Before emigrating to Australia in 1967, they lived in Cheshire, where both sang in the choir at St Andrews, a small stone church in the town of Macclesfield. They still periodically attend church and, as Bill says, 'We have a simple belief in God.' They referred to the poltergeist as 'our friend', a 'friend' who also liked the occasional game of pool. During the decade of activity the couple heard balls whizzing round their pool table and dropping into the pockets. The game always stopped when Bill opened the door to the games room. Dot grinned when she recalled the story and said they used to sit up in bed and laugh: 'He's at it again.' Occasionally Dot saw the 'old feller', who used to shuffle round the house. She described 'him' as a grey outline of the head and shoulders, which invariably gave her the feeling of being stared at. The outline quickly disappeared when eye contact was established.

One night in 1976 the whole family was awakened by a commotion in the kitchen, as if pots and pans were being thrown around. Bill described the incident as 'like a couple of dogs having a mad scrap without the growls'. Yet, when he nervously investigated—anticipating the worst—the pandemonium stopped immediately. Bill was amazed: there was no obvious disturbance in the kitchen; all the crockery and cutlery remained in place. When their only daughter, Rosemary, married in 1983 the frequency of the disturbances diminished. They finally ceased when their youngest son left home in 1988.

Another case I investigated centred on the former RAAF museum building at Point Cook, near Melbourne. The old wooden structure was vulnerable to both fire and vandalism, so the RAAF had installed a sophisticated alarm system. It seemed to make little difference: at times there was as much activity by 'unseen demons' at night, behind the bolted doors, as there was during the working day. The staff nicknamed the 'demon' Dickie and he demonstrated his talents by playing pranks on the exasperated staff. In the old World War I section there was a comprehensive display of mannequins, protected by perspex cabinets. On the night of 16 February 1983, in a daunting display of psychic prowess, virtually all the heavy cabinets were moved against the wall, some metres away, with their free-standing mannequins still in their original positions. This was also the day of the terrible Ash Wednesday bushfires, which turned Melbourne skies into darkness with suffocating smoke and ash. The museum staff were even more mystified because the ash had found its way into the museum, yet there were no tell-tale footprints and no sign of the large cabinets having been moved. It took the staff all day to put the cabinets and mannequins back in their original positions. RAAF police were called to investigate the disturbances but left totally baffled. There was no sign of illegal entry and the alarm had not activated.

And how do we explain the moving gun case? The case was filled with hand guns, rifles, a Bren gun, and a Browning machine gun. It weighs about 100 kilograms and, although mounted on castors, requires a hefty shove to move it. On two occasions this huge cabinet was found to have been moved about a metre and jammed up against an adjacent bookcase. Again, RAAF police were called in, and they decided to mark the position of the legs. The staff found it had moved once more and the matter was made the subject of a police security report. In March 1990 Corporal Steve Durston found unknown forces at work. At the time a rugged 25-year-old who totally dismissed the idea of 'psychic forces', he had to think twice after what follows. One evening, as usual, he locked the museum after a thorough security inspection. The next morning he opened up the museum and carried out his standard check of museum property. He found that a cabinet holding a heavy 1916 Vickers machine gun had moved 3 metres and was jammed up against the wall.

On another occasion a padlocked bolt was undone on one of the inner doors in the museum. The heavy door was behind a showcase that housed model aircraft and weighed at least 110 kilograms. When the staff arrived in the morning they found the heavy door swinging freely. By this stage the RAAF police were becoming wary about investigating incidents in the museum, and some were 'less than enthusiastic' about entering the building at night. The curator of the museum at that time, Warrant Officer Dave Gardner, and his full-time assistant, Corporal Dick Cluley, were extremely sceptical about ghosts or any aspect of psychic phenomena, but they were forced to re-examine their scepticism after what had gone on in the museum.

One disbelieving senior officer thought cadets from the former RAAF Academy were responsible but, because the museum was fitted with the sophisticated alarm system, it is difficult to see how anyone could have entered the building without triggering the alarms. In any case, why would cadets be so irresponsible as to turn on the museum's hot water urn and let it run dry or open a door and so allow intruders to steal objects of genuine historical value? Cadets who entered the Academy were chosen not only for their potential as pilots, engineers, or navigators but also for their integrity. Cadets are notorious for pranks, but usually with a sense of fun, not for malicious damage.

Among other incidents at the museum, books were found on the floor after they had been securely placed on shelves; lights were turned on after a security inspection; the alarm was activated, apparently by remote control; a practice bomb protected by a security rope was moved a metre; and a replica study of the 'father of the Air Force', the late Air Marshal Sir Richard Williams, was tampered with. The Sir Richard Williams display was one of the highlights of the museum. Staff had painstakingly re-created the study, using original furniture. A model, dressed in one of the Air Marshal's mess kits, sits on a chair at his desk. The whole display is protected by a perspex shield and it is impossible to enter the display area without dismantling the perspex. Yet one arm on the model had been moved in such a way as to create a less-than-friendly gesture, the lights on the display had been turned on, and during the two days in which the Air Marshal's mess kit was being dry-cleaned and repaired the alarm was set off. To cap it all, an electric heater that had been unplugged and switched off, was found plugged in and switched on.

On another occasion, the librarian had taken a book from the Dickie Williams display library to use it for research. The following morning the book was back in its position in the library. In addition, a heater that had been built in behind a false wall—because it wasn't needed while a particular display was presented—was turned on. During a routine inspection RAAF police noticed an unusual 'glow' through a museum window and the following morning staff had to tear down the false wall to turn the heater off.

And when former fighter pilot Squadron Leader Jeremy Clark became Commanding Officer of the museum 'someone' was there just to prove that 'hidden helpers' or 'poltergeists' do exist. The museum staff were having hassles with a cantankerous oil heater in the uniform gallery. SQNLDR Clark arrived at work on a cold morning in early June 1990 and immediately tried to fire up the old-fashioned heater. Before start-up it is essential to turn on the oil, air and electric fan. Jeremy spent ten minutes fiddling with the heating device, without success. Frustrated, he nevertheless followed the correct procedures and switched off the oil, air and electricity before turning to his staff and saying, 'We need to get the bloody thing fixed again.' Within half an hour one of his staff asked his boss if he had fixed the heater. He told him no, but was incredulous when he found the heater burning merrily away—especially since the oil, electricity and air were all turned off! Ever the meticulous flier, Jeremy decided 'fate' might not be reliable and turned on the three switches while his staff all stared at the heater and said in unison, 'Dickie's at it again.'

One of the best-documented cases, occurred during 1967 and 1968 at the office of a prominent lawyer in the German town of Rosenheim. Again, it involves a young woman, 19-year-old Anne-Marie Schneider. Put briefly, it started with mysterious phone calls and frequent breakdowns in the mains fuses. Then pictures moved, lamps swayed and occasionally exploded, automatic fuses were blown, developing fluid in the photocopying machine was spilled, drawers opened by themselves, sharp bangs were heard, fluorescent tubes were twisted through 90 degrees in their sockets, and even a large storage cabinet weighing more than 100 kilograms was moved away from a wall.

The lawyer became increasingly irritated: he suspected sabotage and filed a formal charge with the police against the mischief maker. The police were baffled, and the local phone- and power-maintenance staff were brought in to track down the problems. They used monitoring equipment to check the power and installed automatic counters for the phones. The electrical engineers were baffled by large and inexplicable power surges; the phone technicians noted an impossibly high number of outgoing calls to the 'speaking clock' service: in one instance, 46 calls were made to the speaking clock in 15 minutes.

Drastic action was called for, and Professor Hans Bender, a parapsychologist from the University of Freiburg, and two physicists from the Max Planck Institute for Plasmaphysics in Munich were called in to investigate. Bender soon realised that the activity seemed to occur only when Anne-Marie was in the building. He found, for example, when she walked along a corridor lamps hanging from the ceiling would start to swing with increasing force, something he captured on film. For their part, the two physicists noted the same extraordinary power surges as had the electrical engineers. Systematically, they eliminated possible causes, even the X-ray equipment operated by a dentist in the same building, but they found no answers.

After an exhaustive investigation Bender was finally convinced that poltergeist activity was being generated by the young woman. Anne-Marie, distressed about being implicated, was sent home on leave. When she left the goings-on ceased. Bender's conclusion was supported by interviews with more than 40 witnesses who testified to experiencing inexplicable things. When Anne-Marie went to a new place of work, activity began again, but with fewer theatrics; then it slowly died away.

This is another case that supports the theory that the phenomena relate to a person, rather than a location. It aroused considerable interest and was investigated in depth by police and journalists in an attempt to prove fraud. No evidence was found, and it is reported that Anne-Marie is now happily married with children and has not experienced further incidents. Although it was reported that an earlier relationship with a bowling enthusiast broke down when the pins in the bowling alley started behaving erratically!

Professor Bender has his own theory of poltergeist activity:

> If one supposed that objects which penetrate a closed space are transformed into a form of energy which has no more interaction with the components of the closed space (for example, the transformation of neutrons), then transformations of energy would be necessary which far surpass those of the hydrogen bomb. Also, re-materialisation of the original form without any deformation would be inconceivable. Perhaps the hypothesis of higher space, or a fourth dimension, should be considered. One of the physicists with whom I correspond pointed out the possibilities of the old hypothesis of higher space, or the notion of space, which allows a fourfold freedom of movement. Clearly, no room is closed if an object can take a trajectory in higher space. It will, in addition, appear or disappear instantaneously. There is no 'a priori' argument against higher space but there seems to be no evidence from other fields of science in its favour. Ernest Mach, the famous German physicist, discussed it in the beginning of this century as a purely mathematical conception but added that the appearance and disappearance of objects would be the best evidence for a higher dimensionality of space.

A Spanish case investigated in the 1930s revealed none of the characteristics traditionally associated with poltergeists: it simply involved a 'voice'. Known as the 'Saragossa ghost', the 'voice' was first heard speaking down a stove pipe in a flat inhabited by a family named Palazon, in Calle Gascon de Gotor, Saragossa. It was heard by dozens of people, including police and doctors. At times the 'voice' would talk almost incessantly, answering questions when required and at other times asking it's own. The 'agent' for the 'voice' appeared to be the family's 16-year-old maid, Maria Pascuela, because when the police evicted the family and waited up all night nothing happened. When the family returned, with Maria, so did the 'voice.' The police refused to be beaten and placed guards against every stove-pipe outlet that could be used as speaking tube. No result. Finally, a magistrate conducted an inquiry but on 3 December 1934 the 'voice' said its last piece and departed forever. The mystery was never solved.

One of the most remarkable cases that supports the phenomena associated with Liz Fleming involves an investigation by former lecturer in educational psychology at Cardiff University Professor David Fontana. As mentioned, I met Professor Fontana in India in February 1994, and I later read about this case in Jean Ritchie's book, *Inside the Supernatural*.

The case centres around poltergeist activity at a small lawnmower-repair service in the Cathays area of Cardiff. Apart from throwing 'rocks', the poltergeist, nicknamed 'Pete the Polt', was also capable of manifesting pennies, one pound coins and five and ten pound notes. Ninety pounds had appeared. The case is interesting because of the meticulous research carried out by Professor Fontana, who personally experienced some of the activities. The mower business was run by John Mathews and his wife Pat, with assistance from Pat's brother Fred Cook and his wife Gerry. Apparently, Fred was one of 'Pete's favourites, although staff, as well as a number of outsiders, experienced activity. Stone throwing came first. The staff became so irritated by the sound of rocks continually hitting the corrugated roof that they called the local police. The police found nothing. Next, rock-throwing began inside the workshop and each worker suspected another. Eventually they all put their hands on the counter so no one could cheat, but still it continued. The fascinating thing is that the poltergeist appears to have been intelligent: Richard, one of the staff, said they should start noting the evidence and immediately a pen appeared on the counter. And then they started asking for mower parts—a spark plug or big end—and it would appear. This, of course, is similar to my experience of asking for a torch.

Among other phenomena the staff witnessed were bolts materialising in mid-air; cutlery being taken out of drawers and spread on the table (almost as though 'Pete' was trying to set the table, said Ritchie); cutlery being bent; and paper and paper clips materialising to order (the paper often seemed to have come from offices above the shop, where an accountant had his business). Distinctive teaspoons from a restaurant a few doors away also turned up on the staircase at Fred and Gerry's home. On one occasion, Pat challenged 'Pete' to produce a dirty paintbrush—one that did not belong to them arrived at her feet. Pat used to get particularly upset when stones were thrown around her while she was in a locked toilet: 'I don't like the idea of him being in there with me.' She also mentioned that 'Pete' played with her hair. On four occasions Fred saw an apparition in the workshop: a boy aged about nine or ten dressed in clothing typical of a the 1940 or 1950s. On the last occasion, he saw the 'boy' standing in the workshop, waving to him; he tried to engage the 'figure' in conversation but it disappeared.

As Ritchie said, two things rule out the possibility of faking. First, no one in the family had any motive for creating the phenomena and all carefully avoided publicity. Second, the incidents occurred over a six-year period and there were so many witnesses there can be no question of one person faking it all.

Professor Fontana, meanwhile, was relentless in his investigations, considering such possibilities as underground water, vibrations of traffic, even disturbances in the building. He went to the workshop on numerous occasions and never saw anything to suggest trickery. I found his comments of particular importance and very relevant to my own research.

> It is the sheer volume of activity and the number of witnesses, many of whom I have tracked down and

interviewed, that make it special. Poltergeists sometimes will not perform in front of anyone except the inhabitants of the house or building and investigators have to take a great deal on trust. That has been partly true with 'Pete.' I have sometimes gone to the workshop when John has rung to say there was a lot of activity only to find nothing happens when I am there, but I have been able to witness actual phenomena. I was also intrigued by my own reactions. When I was there, I would eliminate all possibilities of fraud or natural causes and would know that I was seeing genuine phenomena. But as soon as I was away from the premises and reflecting on what I had seen, I would find myself trying to reject the evidence of my own senses by coming up with all sorts of tortuous rationales for what was happening.

Liz believes the 'intelligence' can read her mind. And she is very confident of the answers given through taps on a hard surface or 'vocal noises'. Historically there are a number of cases supporting Liz, including an Irish case in 1877. Sir William Barrett mentally asked a poltergeist to tell him, through taps, how many fingers he had open while his hands were hidden in the side pockets of his overcoat. We presume of course the integrity of the subject, but Sir William changed the number of his open fingers four times and the poltergeist was correct each time, although no word was spoken during the experiment.

Liz also believes she can communicate with her spirit friend Matt by way of a code she has devised. She has to telephone a particular friend, who provides 'extra power'. The friend hears only Liz's voice. The code is as follows: one tap means 'yes', two 'no', three 'sometimes', four 'maybe', five 'I'll try', and six 'don't know'. Liz says Matt devised his own method of contact when he was happy, or else she had guessed it, by using continual tapping sounds. 'I tried to look at every possibility to see if I was being tricked or fooled', she said.

I had my television on the table not far from the telephone and would turn the TV down so I could hear Matt tapping. I would ask him 'Okay Matt, if you're so smart, what's on telly now?' I would give him three choices; he always picked the correct program. I would take something from my cupboard and sit it on the table and ask him to tap after I had named a few items: he was always correct.

Occasionally Liz is able to contact on the phone other spirit friends she names as Rosco and Ben. With this pair she is able to clearly distinguish words. The sceptic would argue that Liz is only hearing the reply through her imagination. Yet, if it can be scientifically proved, it opens up a whole new world in the field of psychic research. Will we be able to pick up a 'psychic' telephone and speak to the deceased? Paranormal research is indeed exciting.

12
Caressa has the final word

I want people to know I'm proud of being a prostitute. I really believe prostitutes provide a valuable community service because we look after the lonely and perverted so they don't impose their will on innocent children or women. I treat my clients as friends. I believe what I do is an art and I love being good at what I do. I am one of God's children and I know He looks after me. I believe in destiny and this is my destiny.

I also recognise that I am going to be condemned for my communication with the spirits. I wish I could prove their existence to the whole world. However, spirits are intimately tied up with religious beliefs and are mostly understood by way of faith. Paranormal activities and things of that nature are the only way to bridge the gap between faith and everyday reality. I am lucky to have had the benefit of such experiences. Many, including Ken Llewelyn, have already put their personal integrity and reputation on the line to document these cases. It takes considerable courage, in the face of losing all credibility, for these individuals to pursue their research and present the truth to the public. I believe if intelligent, open-minded individuals find I lack credibility, then the experiences of the witnesses presented in my case should be examined. My spirits are a miracle of nature, just like life itself. They are the closest thing to God I can achieve. Like most of us, I believe the physical and spiritual world are usually kept separate, except in my case, where a communication link has been established.

Too many people are only familiar with the old stories of ghosts or spirits and how they haunt people and places. These people's beliefs are often based on ignorance because they haven't been lucky enough to be in my shoes. I trust these spirits with my soul. There are no words powerful enough to describe the feelings I have for my friends. I know they are dead and they know they are dead, too, but I communicate with them as though they are alive in the physical world. I am constantly learning through these communications. Often this makes me frustrated, because I have always been impatient—I want things to happen *now*! On the other hand, I appreciate and respect what I believe is a gift from God, or the powers that be. I am not religious and have only read two books relating to the spiritual world.

What has happened to me has been described by my spirits 'as a coincidence, an accident'. I can only pray that I will be given the benefit of the doubt: I am not so stupid or ignorant that I cannot also see the absurdity surrounding the chain of events experienced with my spirits. I wish that everybody would accept that we are all miracles and by observing the world around us we should expand our awareness. This will inevitably bring us to the conclusion of how little we know. Life is precious and so is death. I, too, need constant proof from my spirits and I continually push for more in the hope that I will get the answers that I am looking for. Funnily enough, I'm also a sceptic, and I often listen with disbelief to other people's accounts of contact with the spirit world. But my spirits have proved to me that life is eternal. I personally wish that once we are dead, that's that—I don't like the idea of reincarnation. I would prefer to leave the world and not return.

Although I have a belief in the spirit world, this should not make me a candidate for the kind of dysfunctional problems I could so easily be accused of. Anyway, if you still question my sanity, then believe, as I've said before, my witnesses.

It hasn't always been peace and harmony: on occasion I've felt real terror in my dealings with the spirit world. At one stage I was urged by the Catholic Church to discontinue my association. I tried for several months, but my curiosity became too strong and I reverted. It is another world, one that is very much alive, here on this planet but in another dimension or 'something like that', as my spirits say.

My conversations with my spirits are personal. They tell me that to publicly advertise our communications is 'dangerous'. I share only a small sample of my communication with outsiders, and until I gain credibility and confidence, if ever, I will not give out further information—I fear embarrassment and ridicule from a disbelieving society. The time is not yet right. I have never been prepared for what they do and I am constantly enlightened by their antics. I believe their abilities are endless.

Throughout my life I have suffered emotional stress, primarily through my desire to be slim and beautiful, which created severe bulimic and anorexic disturbances that wasted 14 years of my life. During those years I didn't live: I existed, and I often wished I were dead. Still a dark cloud hangs over my head. Suicide became my friend and, like a good friend, I wanted to be with her as often as possible. I have tried to take my life more than 20 times and I am still suicidal sometimes.

I am wary because my spirits have shown me what it is like to die and say themselves, 'It is no better where we are. Sometimes it's good and sometimes it's bad.' They have told me we were never intended to take our own lives. But, in spite of their advice and all the therapy I have had over the years, I will still choose to die on my own terms. I thank God that I have been able to retain my desire to live through plastic surgery. This has given me the confidence to continue and I know I look better than most other women of my age.

The time will come when I no longer have the desire to continue. I have already decided where I will take my life. No one will find me this time. I don't want to be rescued because I believe it's my choice. I'll smoke a few cigarettes, drink half a bottle of Scotch and swallow 200 or 300 Anafranil tablets. I can almost feel the relief as I inhale the smoke, the soporific effects of the alcohol numbing my brain, and allow myself to drift off into a more peaceful world. And then, I hope, I'll find out the truth.

For Liz suicide brings enlightenment

I didn't know when I transcribed Caressa' words how prophetic they were. I remember Liz's partner berating her when she insisted that her description of her preferred method of suicide should remain. I tried to defuse the argument and told Liz she should think about it because the 'offending' words could easily be removed. But Liz was adamant—nothing should be changed.

Although she was now 41 years old, Liz still found it easy to attract clients. She told newcomers on the phone that she was 25, and her voluptuous body, moulded with more than $50 000 worth of plastic surgery, ensured that excited younger clients did not question the fact. Her lively, sensual personality and rapier wit also attracted more mature and intelligent men. But Liz knew prostitution was taking its toll. The tight, shiny skin on her face suggested one too many facelifts, and a bald spot hiding beneath her long blonde hair made her paranoid about ageing. She postponed the inevitable by turning to even more bizarre experiments with her spirit friends. She finally gave up prostitution after a series of what she termed 'evil' psychic attacks. It was not an easy transition: she had built up a very successful business and, although she changed her phone number, clients would still turn up at her front door demanding her services.

Typically, Liz became totally focused on her next challenge—ridding herself of this 'invasion' of her mind with all the resources she could muster. She 'verbally assaulted' every Catholic priest she could find in an attempt to extricate herself from this 'madness': she told me she approached more than ten priests before one finally listened to her desperate pleas for help. For a short time, with the assistance of a Catholic councillor, she took to the Bible's teachings as avidly as she had to prostitution, but time was running out. Her partner supported her in her decision to seek comfort in the Bible—after all, it was he who had seriously considered a career as a Dominican priest.

Sadly, after years of suffering fits, he was diagnosed as having a brain tumour. The last time I saw them together was during a visit to Canberra Hospital, prior to the operation, in early 1997. Liz was half asleep across Johnny's bed when I arrived that evening, but she pulled herself up and greeted me in a dazed state. Moments later Johnny awoke from what I imagine was a drug-induced sleep and, in spite of his life hanging in the balance, greeted me in his usual affable way. I spoke to them for 15 minutes or so. In spite of the doctor's black prognosis, Johnny was positive about the outcome. He had no doubt that he would pull through. And Liz, allowing negative thoughts to enter her mind, said with conviction that if he died she would take her own life, so that they could be together again. They held hands and dreamed of living together without the pall of prostitution hanging over their heads.

Each spoke positively of the future ... of moving away from Canberra, of buying a house 'down the coast'. But there was a terrible web of sadness: the 'gods of fate' were dealing their final hand. I was intruding, so I didn't stay long. Theirs was a relationship that defied logic. A prostitute in her early forties and a very likeable young man in his mid-twenties. People who knew them often failed to understand the genuine affection between them. Certainly, their relationship was not a bed of roses: the impulsive Liz threw Johnny out a number of times, but the next minute she was on the phone begging him to come back. And he always returned, in spite of considerable pressure from his parents.

Johnny survived his operation but needed constant post-operative care because he was having terrible seizures. Liz always admitted she didn't handle stress or responsibility well, and looking after her sick partner and coping with her changing life was becoming an overwhelming burden. A month or so before I went on my long service leave to the United Kingdom in June 1997 Liz rang me and we spoke at length about the book. We had previously agreed to put the book aside because of her new-found faith.

But during our conversation she confessed that her counselling had produced few long-term benefits. She was surprisingly level headed, though, and continually repeated that the book should be published. I reminded her that I would be overseas for eight months and would ring her on my return to arrange the final edit. Again, I was taken aback by her lack of concern about the delay—unusual for Liz because she was such an impatient person. She reiterated that she wanted to see the book published since it contained important messages. She had read every draft and was well aware it was not all spiritual thoughts and high-mindedness. Her measured voice was at odds with her attitude during our early research, when she used to repeat with bizarre intensity that the book would make her famous! She even chose American star Sharon Stone to play her part when her story was made into a film. Her confidence—which at times verged on hysteria—was a little wearing but she never wavered.

Unfortunately, I did not take note of the date: Liz rang me so often. Many a time she infuriated me because, even on a short trip away, she would fill the one-hour tape on my answering machine and friends would complain that they couldn't leave a message. I overlooked the terrible portent of that conversation: it was the last 'earthly' one I had with Liz. Looking back, I am sure she deliberately planned those last words. For Liz, they were far too measured.

When I returned to Australia in February 1998 I spent a frustrating month trying to phone Liz and track her movements through friends and acquaintances. Then I contacted the police and her social worker, but without success. Finally, I jumped on my Triumph and rode to her house. When I knocked, a very nervous woman opened the door. I guess her state was understandable: I was dressed in leathers and, for all I knew, ex-clients might still be coming to the door. I told her I wanted to know where the previous owner was. The woman replied that the previous owner had taken her own life and quickly closed the door. I walked down the driveway feeling terrible, jumped on the bike, and left Liz's house for the last time. With a final backward glance, I wondered if that woman had any idea of what had happened in that house.

When I returned I rang medium Monica Hamers because she too was trying to find Liz. We spoke at length about Liz: in spite of her very obvious foibles, we both liked her. We had a 'phone wake' as we recalled her outrageous tales and her outlandish sense of humour. When I hung up I felt my grief somewhat assuaged. Yes, like many others, I was not surprised that she took her own life, but that did not help with the final realisation that she was gone. Monica and I agreed that when the time was right we should try and contact Liz. If anyone were to try to 'talk' with us from the 'other side' it would be the very determined and single-minded Liz!

The evidence I gleaned suggests that Liz's suicide was carefully planned. This was consistent with a suicide attempt she'd made after her marriage break-up. She told me that the attempt had been 'planned to the last detail' but for some reason, which she could not explain, did not go ahead. Before becoming a prostitute, Liz had had a successful career as a secretary. She proudly showed me references from two noted Australian professors and a rather prophetic one from an assistant director-general of the Department of Social Security, who said, 'I am sure she will give her best efforts in any vocational situation.'

Ever the meticulous secretary, Liz wrote personal letters to a number of friends and sold her car and household items. From what I can gather, at around 9 pm on Friday 25 July she went to the local chemist to buy sleeping tablets. She then walked to the field where her horse was agisted. Along the way she was offered a lift home by concerned police, but she insisted she was fine and told them she simply wanted to feed her horse. More than 24 hours later she was found dead, her favourite horse lying next to her. Liz was just 42.

In April 1998 Monica rang me and said that Liz had been in her thoughts and we should make the attempt. What follows is an edited transcript of our 'conversation' with 'Liz' while Monica was in deep trance. There was no angelic language from the 'contact'—it seemed as though earthly Liz was back in action!

Liz's first comments:

> I thought it was all bullshit, but it's true. When I came out of my body I met Marty and many others who were waiting for me. But then it is important to make people understand about spirit life being real, life after death being real and people being responsible for their own actions. People have to return to the world, and look what a mess it is! I thought I was happy and I wasn't—always took drugs because I wanted to accept what I was doing. I was holding onto the spirits because I wanted them to be my friend, to feel like I was different from other people. I wanted to be special and I really didn't believe what I was being told. I feel I made a contribution. I achieved something so people won't forget about me any more. [I presume she meant through the book.]. I wanted people to remember me as beautiful. My spirit is beautiful and I didn't know till I got here how beautiful I am. I look really young and I've got a lovely face and I'm surrounded by pretty colours like a butterfly. I thought that I was nothing, that I wasted my life and did stupid things. Now I understand that the part I had to play was to help people who are on the wrong pathway.
>
> People think they are nobody, but they have to understand that everyone can do things and be special; everyone has

> abilities and it doesn't matter how close you are to the bottom. Marty, for example, had AIDS, and some of the guys were really sick in what they did, but there is no judgment here. Because it's not what you think, life is not what you think. Being over here is not what you think. It could be different if I really work at it because I've done the worst of my sufferings and being crazy in my head. Now I can look at improving.

In answer to a question about the content of the book, Liz replied,

> Most of the stuff in the book is fine, but what I need to get across is that people from the other side want you to know they are there, that they can live with you and be caring. I, for example, visit my partner often because he is very sick. I want to tell people that I understand more about God now and it's all bullshit that this religion is right and the other is wrong. I want people to understand that I really cared for clients and wanted to help them. I wasn't there just to take the money for nothing. But what I did was bad for my spirit and bad for my body. Everyone needs to know that ordinary people have a soul and a spirit and they are all beautiful. They need to know spirits are your friends and that they can change your thinking. It's true that their voices can come to you if you are close to them. They can make things appear and disappear and it's nothing to be frightened of. If you believe in God and you do it from your heart then nothing bad can come to you.

Do you regret taking up prostitution?

> The spirit shines through all, because everyone is beautiful underneath. People need to know the truth that you can be a prostitute in one life and a priest in another. It was a good lesson because I learnt a lot of things and it was part of the experience of growing. I learnt a lot about human nature and why people are so weak.

Do you regret committing suicide?

> I always knew when the time came I would have to leave. I

wasn't scared, it wasn't violent. It was very peaceful and everyone was waiting for me. I'm not sorry: I couldn't live any more. My work was finished because I couldn't help my sons or my partner and I wanted to be with my friends. I'm sorry about my sons because I was a bit crazy and had too many hang-ups. I used drugs so I could root ugly old people and sometimes I didn't know what I was doing or what I was saying.

Were you dealing with evil forces?

Sometimes I was scared. Some religious people I spoke to wanted to make the good spirits into the devil. Some of my customers had dark things they left in my house. Other spirits were earthbound and they just wanted to be close to me.

Could you describe the process of your of suicide?

I lay down next to my horse and it was like drifting in a mist of pretty colours. I was trying to get through, calling to Marty to come and get me, and then everything became a big bright light. I could see Marty and others and they were waiting for me to come. They said 'Come quickly, Liz. Come quickly. Don't look back.' So I was stupid. I tried to get up and couldn't stand. They said, 'No, no, no! Leave that behind. Run. Get out, get out!' And I thought 'What are they talking about? My legs won't work. I can't stand up, and I'm all over the place.' Then they pulled me towards them and I felt that I was a piece of light, and then I was there with them. And they said, 'Don't look back, Liz, don't look back. Hold on tight to us.'

They brought me through this shimmering doorway and pulled me out the other side. And I thought, 'Shit, what's this place?' They said, 'It's OK, sit down. Sit down and just hold tight to us.' Then after a while I thought, 'I feel strong. My arms and legs are fine.' I felt good and got up, shook my hair and tidied myself. I said, 'Well, I'm here, I'm OK, I'm not dead' and they laughed at me They said, 'You are here on the other side, but you've got to get used to this body. Don't look back at the other one.'

Then I didn't remember anything more and I went into a deep sleep. When I woke I saw this bright light of pale green and beautiful gold colours. I found myself alone, standing in front of this big light. It was like God was asking me questions but there was nothing there but the light. I thought about my stuffed-up life, about everything that happened. I don't understand a lot of it, but I know I've been back a couple of times driving around as though I was here (earthbound). I'm not very consistent and feel ungrounded because I think about things then I'm gone. I don't really know where I'm supposed to stay but I think I'm going to have to be born again.

It's always preached that one shouldn't commit suicide.

Well, it's not right to snuff yourself out and it's not right to hang yourself, but I knew I was going to do it and they knew I was going to do it. It was very gentle, as though I had been preparing myself for years. It's not good finishing your life early because you don't learn your responsibilities, but my body was no good.

You don't regret committing suicide?

No. It was just a matter of time.

Do you recognise yourself as you would be on earth?

My face is perfect and more serene and my hair is perfect.

What are you learning on the other side?

First, I have to learn to have control over my thinking. I'm learning that I have a part to play and things to achieve, but I've had other different lives. I thought I was just a no-good prostitute but I wasn't like that before. In a past life I was once a pretty boy playing a drum, but I didn't live very long. In another life I was in a position of wealth and power and was unkind to people under me. Because of this I had to learn a life of suffering and servitude to make up for what I did to other people. Now I am learning about spiritual truths, about discipline of thought, discipline of action and responsibilities. They also talk about where you have evolved to the point where you could consider being reborn. They teach about the physical and spiritual worlds. Although I have gone to a better place my journey is continuing. They talk about a better environment for children, about the futility of drugs, and the danger of destroying ourselves.

Then, in the middle of this question-and-answer session, 'Liz' ceased to take any notice of my questions and her voice became very animated.

I'll tell you what I saw, I saw the Madonna. I saw her coming down the pathway and she was dressed in white and she had such a bright light around her and she said, 'Come to me, my child, come to me for you are just as worthy as any other and I love you just the same. You are my daughter, my child.' And then she said, 'Don't worry any more about your past, but know that you are a child of mine and I will comfort you.' I was so scared of her I wanted to hide away in a corner because I was unclean, but she said, 'Being with me will purify you, you will forgive yourself and I will forgive you. You must let go of your earth life and forget. Just be what you are and come with me.'

I felt so good, so beautiful and so wonderful just for that time. To know that she was so caring and loving and that I had such a wonderful experience with her before she went away. Then I had to go back for more work and learning. I want to feel as though I can go in front of God and justify what I have done without feeling that I have worked for the devil to get there.

The session ended with 'Liz' saying,

I dedicate this book to my life and to truth. People need to know that nothing is wasted and nothing is in vain, that underneath everything is beautiful and everything is good. And if you believe in this you will be protected and you will find peace, a peace I found so elusive. I want people to know they have to journey to many places to find the truth. They musn't let anything stop them.

I've replayed the tape many times and, although Monica knew Liz well and could obviously 'make up' information that reflected Liz's life, I don't believe this was so. Monica was in deep trance and was unaware of the words she spoke. What interested me most was the total change that came across the medium during 'Liz's' recall of the meeting with the Madonna. I have seen Monica in trance probably a 100 times, but I have never seen her so animated. The enthusiasm was pure Liz!

Was it her personality coming through Monica? Realistically I don't now. 'Her' comment about 'her' face and hair was spot on: Liz was very concerned about her looks and always wanted to be beautiful. But there was also a very spiritual side to Liz. She always spoke earnestly about the publication of this book and its purpose of demonstrating that there is 'life beyond life'. At the same time she recognised, and indeed encouraged, the need to use graphic language and stories to ensure the book would be read. To be sure, it is sensational in parts, but in these days of 'information overload', a hammer is sometimes needed where a feather would have sufficed 50 years ago.

I put forward Liz's story in the hope that one day we will all learn the truth of the ultimate conundrum: whether we continue in a vital form after our three score years and ten.

Bibliography

Bibliography

Australian Penthouse 1996, November.

Branden, Victoria 1980, *Understanding Ghosts*, Victor Gollancz, London.

Cooper, Joe 1989, *Modern Psychic Experiences*, Robert Hale, London.

Ellis, Havelock 1937, *The Psychology of Sex*, fourth impression, William Heinemann, London.

Evans, Hiliary 1979, *The Oldest Profession*, David & Charles, Newton Abbot, London.

Fortean Times 1998, 'Stone' November.

Gauld, A. & Cornell A.D. 1979, *Poltergeists*, Routledge & Kegan Paul, London.

Good Weekend 1998, 13 June.

Inglis, Brian 1986, *The Paranormal*, Paladin Grafton Books, London.

International Express 1994, 16–22 March.

Jung, Carl 1973, *Memories, Dreams, Reflections*, Pantheon Books, New York.

Langone, John 1980, *Like, Love, Lust*, Little Brown & Co., Boston.

Litchfield Times 1998, 9, 18, 23, 30 April, 7 May.

marie claire 1997, September.

marie claire 1999, January.

Northern Territory News 1998, 14, 16, 17 April, 29 November, 14 December.

Philip, Neil 1991, *Working Girls*, Bloomsbury Publishing, London.

Price, Harry 1994, *Poltergeist*, University of London Library, London.

Ritchie, Jean 1992, *Inside the Supernatural*, Harper Collins, London.

Scott, George Ryley 1968, *History of Prostitution*, Random House, London.

Thurlow, David 1992, *Profumo*, Robert Hale, London.

Underwood, Peter 1984, *This Haunted Isle*, Harrap, London.

Watson, Lyall 1986, *Beyond Supernature*, Hodder & Stoughton, London.

Watson, Lyall 1992, *Supernature II*, Hodder & Stoughton, London.

Weekend Australian 1999, 26–27 June.